Kentucky
Folkmusic

Kentucky Folkmusic

An Annotated Bibliography

BURT FEINTUCH

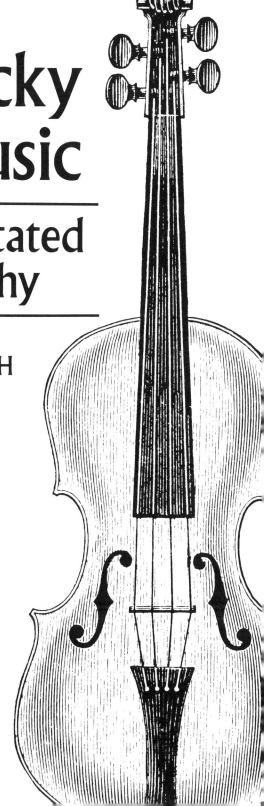

THE UNIVERSITY PRESS
OF KENTUCKY

Library of Congress Cataloging in Publication Data

Feintuch, Burt, 1949-
  Kentucky folkmusic.

  Includes indexes.
  1. Folk music—Kentucky—Bibliography. 2. Folk-songs,
English—Kentucky—Bibliography. I. Title.
ML128.F74F4   1985   016.7817769   85-6225
ISBN 0-8131-1556-6

TO MAX

Contents

Acknowledgments

Bibliography can be an onerous task. The burden of this one was lightened considerably by the help and support of a number of people and institutions. First and foremost are the folklore graduate assistants at Western Kentucky University who, over the years, were both gracious and methodical in their help. I am very grateful to Luanne Glynn, Steve Hutchinson, Cathy Hanby-Sikora, Julie Hauri-Foster, Tom Kozma, Ann Taft, and Chris Werth. They will, I imagine, be almost as happy as I to see that this project has reached completion. I also owe special thanks to D.K. Wilgus and Charles Wolfe, two of the foremost scholars of Kentucky's musical traditions. Each has played an important part in kindling and renewing my enthusiasm for Kentucky's music, and both were kind enough to share important materials of their own with me, providing a number of very helpful leads and annotations.

Western Kentucky University has been generous, awarding me a summer research stipend to support a preliminary bibliographic survey and later following that with a sabbatical which afforded me the time to do the bulk of the annotations. Susan Tucker, of Western's interlibrary loan department, kept her good humor, and so did Elona Sabo, who typed the manuscript. The Kentucky Folklife Foundation granted funds to help with typing costs. Staff members at the libraries of the University of Kentucky, Berea College, and the Country Music Foundation were also quite helpful.

Introduction

It is difficult for me to remember when I first linked the terms "folkmusic" and "Kentucky," because to me, just as to many Americans, the two have long seemed in some way connected. For better or worse, Kentucky figures prominently in our national sense of what folkmusic is and where we find it, even though by now we know that virtually every group, every locality and region, sings. Before I was an academic, I was a folkmusic enthusiast; Kentucky's powerful musical traditions were at least broadly familiar to me years before I'd ever set foot in the state—years, in fact, before I was even precisely certain where Kentucky fits on the map. Surely the entire map sings, but in our national consciousness Kentucky may sing just a bit more loudly.

The major achievement in nineteenth-century folksong scholarship, if not in all of that century's folklore research, was the publication of Francis James Child's monumental comparative study *The English and Scottish Popular Ballads*, 5 vols. (1882–98. Reprint. New York: Dover Publications, 1965). Child, a literary scholar at Harvard, was convinced that the ballad was essentially dead, a closed account. Ironically, at virtually the same time as the publication of Child's opus, the nation was becoming increasingly aware that folksong was anything but a literary artifact, and to many it began to seem that Kentucky was especially well endowed with traditional music. In the late 1890s, when Raymond C. Rexford of Berea College brought a group of folksinging students from the Kentucky mountains to a fundraising program, the audience was entranced. (See entry #478.) Although probably not the first to do so, Rexford had discovered what many others have found and what still others regularly rediscover—that Kentucky's grassroots music has remarkable appeal. In the last two centuries a diverse (motley might be a better word) group of people—reformers, enthusiasts, the musically literate and musically illiterate, radicals, liberals, at least one surprising British socialist gentleman and his woman companion, amateurs, local residents, and academics—have been sufficiently captivated by that music to devote considerable energy to harvesting it from its fertile ground.

Paradoxically, a number of sometimes contradictory images have been associated with the music. Some have seen it as the music of a pristine society, lost in its geographic and geological isolation, more a reflection of the England of centuries past than of modern America. Others have regarded the music as a plaintive cry from a region despoiled by the worst of contemporary modern forces—industrialization, greed, lack of regard for culture and environment. To some, it is a music which is unchanging, although to others it is fluid and ever-changing. There are those who believe the music is dying, while another school of thought holds that the music is as vital as ever, perhaps more so. And, of course, there is considerable opinion that only the mountains are musical, even though the weight of books and articles clearly demonstrates that the entire commonwealth has no shortage of traditional song and music.

Is there something inordinate about the way in which Kentucky's traditional music has a resonance that carries far beyond the state's boundaries? Folkmusic, after all, tends not to respect political boundaries, making it quite unlikely that people in Monroe County, Kentucky, have musical repertoires significantly different from those of their neighbors a few miles to the south in Clay County, Tennessee. The Ohio River may serve as something of a stylistic boundary to the north, but in the east and the south, Kentucky's borders are not made of the stuff which locks in anything as enduring as a fiddle style, a ballad text, a spiritual. And, at the same time, there is no homogeneity in style and repertoire across the state. The famous "high lonesome" sound of singing in the mountains of eastern Kentucky is uncommon in the flatlands of the Jackson Purchase. Although it may be almost futile to seek blues singers in the mountains, look in Louisville, in the black communities in southern Kentucky, and there you are likely to find the blues. I can think of nothing which stylistically separates Kentucky's traditional music from that of its neighbors; neither can anyone reasonably claim that the music is uniform across the state. Yet a bibliography of works on folkmusic in Tennessee (Eleanor Goehring, *Tennessee Folk Culture: An Annotated Bibliography* [Knoxville: Univ. of Tennessee Press, 1982]) lists about 175 entries, while this bibliography for Kentucky lists more than 700. Why the difference? The answer lies, I believe, in the way Kentucky's music has periodically been rediscovered and put to various symbolic uses.

A photograph published in 1917 as part of an article entitled "Hunting the Lonesome Tune in the Wilds of Kentucky" portrays two pioneer fieldworkers and is captioned "Loraine Wyman and Howard Brockway invaded the mountainous regions of Kentucky and entered the most isolated regions, in order to obtain strange folksongs for the delectation of more sophisticated audiences" (see #257). Oddly enough, the photograph shows Brockway playing the guitar, while Wyman appears to be doing the singing to a group of mountain children. But if we ignore that incongruity the caption would seem to sum up the early national interest in Kentucky's traditional music. To the academics, the *literati,* and the journalists who were beginning to appreciate that folksong was anything but a closed account, Kentucky was characterized by its otherness. There one collected "strange" folksongs and took them elsewhere for the "delectation of more sophisticated audiences." Somehow, "down there," particularly in the mountains, seemed to exist a society that was backwardly mysterious, isolated, and simultaneously a bit frightening and a bit romantic. Henry Shapiro's *Appalachia on Our Minds* (see #271) masterfully chronicles the not entirely innocent development and manipulation of that image of the entire southern Appalachian region. To that I wish only to add that it appears that, early on, Kentucky seemed to sum up the stereotypical characteristics generally assigned the entire region. Ask any Kentuckian, regardless of generation, who has endured barbs about not wearing shoes to school. To a nation increasingly fascinated by the otherness of a region, Kentucky's folksong was a tangible symbol of another era, another world. And, having once served as such a symbol for a nation discovering its indigenous music, it has been rediscovered and put to similar uses a number of times since.

As I examine the literature of this music, I am not only struck by the chronicles of the pioneer collectors and scholars who during the first decades of the century were apt to write titles of the "Hunting the Lonesome Tune in the Wilds of Kentucky" ilk. I am also impressed that many of the most significant names in the histories of both the folksong revival of the 1950s and 1960s and the emergence of the modern generation of folksong scholars—Lomax, Green, Ritchie, Niles, Seeger, Wilgus, and many others—recur throughout this compendium. When, as it periodically has, the nation's attention turns to its grassroots music—whether it is Wyman and Brockway and their "more sophisticated audiences," or the British fieldworker Cecil J. Sharp, who "discovered" ancient English songs in the eastern highlands, or Josiah Combs writing a 1925 dissertation at the Sorbonne based on his childhood musical traditions in Kentucky, or Archie Green writing of the powerful singer Aunt Molly Jackson, or filmmaker-revivalist-musician John Cohen telling us that eastern Kentucky in the 1960s is reminiscent of the Great Depression, or Charles Wolfe writing about the contribution of Kentucky's grassroots music to the development of modern country music—whenever Americans consider folkmusic, for better or for worse, Kentucky figures in their thoughts.

The 709 books and articles presented here are the cullings of several years spent hunting sources in the wilds of various libraries. At the start, it was obvious that I had to establish certain rules as to what was fair game. I chose not to include certain kinds of materials, mostly because of practicality and my desire to see my work in print before it became outdated. For those reasons, I have not included book reviews or recordings. Records certainly deserve their own reference work, but bibliography and discography are such different skills that I am not the person to compile the latter. Documentary record albums and their notes are unquestionably valuable sources of information about Kentucky's folkmusic. Unfortunately, comprehensive indexes and research collections do not exist for recordings as they do for printed materials. An additional complication is that in order to include recordings in an annotated bibliography I would have had to examine the albums themselves in order to annotate their liner notes. More traditional discographies frequently can be accomplished without having the record on hand, but that would not have been the case for me. Early songsters and hymnals are also potentially valuable sources, but I again decided that they were for the most part beyond my reach and therefore beyond the scope of this book. The same goes for newspaper articles, although I have included those when I encountered them elsewhere. Finally, I found that I had to draw the line when it came to fan publications. Many Kentuckians have built professional careers on their musical roots, and as a consequence they are featured in countless ephemeral publications directed at curious or admiring fans. Although I have included citations from a few magazines which are fan-oriented, I have not found it possible to include most such publications. The citations run through 1983, but such factors as library acquisition schedules and publishers running late prevent me from claiming that this bibliography is complete for 1983 or even 1982.

I also realized early that I would have to develop some sort of defensible definition of folkmusic in order to be able to state clearly what sorts of things are likely to be found in this book. Shortly thereafter I realized the impossibility of drawing a precise line, an exact boundary. To me, folkmusic is community-based music performed and perpetuated for largely noncommercial reasons. If the core of that notion is reasonably straightforward, as I believe it to be, at its edges there are problems. In the twentieth century, the dialectic between the community-based and the mass-mediated has influenced, and in some cases disrupted, local singing and music-making to degrees which we are still discovering. At the edges of my definition are the singers and musicians who were first and foremost community-based musicians but who sought commercial recognition. I have chosen to include references to such performers when it seemed to me that their careers, whether local or international, rest firmly on a community-based music tradition. Hence, Rosine native Bill Monroe, who learned his music from family and neighbors and recast it, creating bluegrass music, is included here, but those Kentuckians who have had successful mass-mediated careers which show little connection to their community's music are not.

Little needs to be said about this book's organization. Each of the eight chapters is organized around a significant concept, and the table of contents should serve as the best map of the territory. Some entries defied absolute categorization and are listed in the chapter which seemed to be the best compromise. They are also listed in the cross-references, a group of which begins each chapter. The three indexes, author, subject, and periodical, should be of additional assistance.

Seven hundred and nine books and articles is a corpus of noteworthy dimensions. Yet it is clear that there remains much work to be done. Kentucky's Anglo-American musical traditions have been sought, presented, and discussed quite considerably. This is particularly so for vocal music, and even more for the ballad. On the other hand, the literature of African-American music in Kentucky, which includes some notable works, has been studied much less thoroughly. Of ethnic music in the commonwealth we still know virtually nothing. Entire genres—such as gospel music, perhaps the most vital of community-based musics—are essentially unexplored. Geographic coverage, too, has been uneven. In the early years collectors and scholars journeyed—physically in the first case, usually metaphorically in the latter—to the mountains. There they sought relics of an ancient English past. The Bluegrass, the Pennyrile, and the Jackson Purchase were initially less exotic, hence less appealing, although each of the state's regions has always had its folkmusic proponents, frequently laboring alone and lovingly. That tradition of looking to the mountains for music, not quite a rule because it has far too many exceptions, has seemingly always exerted its power. Even today the literature of Kentucky's folkmusic leans to the east.

In its biases and its uneven coverage of the subject, the body of literature presented here is, of course, no different from the literature of American folkmusic as a whole. What is striking, though, and remarkable is its bulk, its extent. Kentucky's grassroots music, inextricably bound up in our national aesthetic and imagination, is perhaps the most-chronicled of any state's. Although there is much still to be done, this volume should testify that the scholars, collectors, fieldworkers, enthusiasts, and, most importantly, the singers and musicians have laid an exceptional foundation. There is little reason to doubt that their efforts will continue.

Kentucky
Folkmusic

Collections and Anthologies

Also see entries: #287, 296, 308, 326, 330, 343, 352, 379, 389-90, 392, 398-99, 404-405, 424, 438-41, 444-45, 450, 467, 470, 475, 480, 482, 485-86, 488, 490-93, 494, 500, 510, 547, 565, 579, 581, 598, 641, 645

1. Adams, James Taylor. *Death in the Dark: A Collection of Factual Ballads of American Mine Disasters.* Big Laurel, Va.: Adams-Mullins Press, 1941.
   A collection by a Letcher Countian of songs associated with mining disasters, for the most part in Kentucky, Virginia, and Pennsylvania. No melodies.
2. Amburgey, Don Carlos. "Folk Songs." *Kentucky Folklore Record* 9 (1963): 1-19.
   A collection of songs heard by the author as a child in Kentucky. Words only; no tunes. Texts apparently come from eastern Kentucky. No ballads are presented.
3. Anderson, Faye Scott. "Another Version of 'Pearl Bryan'/'The Jealous Lover.'" *Kentucky Folklore Record* 21 (1975): 119-20.
   Presents fifty-year-old text of a ballad (example of Laws F1, F2, F3) found near Clinton-Cumberland County line.
4. Babb, Harvey A. "Folklore of Kentucky." B.A. thesis, University of Kentucky, 1911.
   Includes a number of ballads "collected from some of the most rural districts of the various counties of Western Kentucky."
5. "Ballads and Rhymes from Kentucky." *Appalachian Heritage* 2, no. 1 (1974): 19-26.
   Five ballads collected in Knott County by Katherine Pettit and published with annotations by G.L. Kittredge in 1907 in the *Journal of American Folklore.* Texts only; no tunes. [See #110.]
6. Beatty, Arthur. "Some Ballad Variants and Songs." *Journal of American Folklore* 22 (1909): 63-71.
   Includes two texts from Kentucky, "The East Kentucky Hills" and "The Returning Soldier."

7. Bonar, Eleanor Jean. "A Collection of Ballads and Popular Songs." M.A. thesis, State University of Iowa, 1930.
About a hundred songs collected by the author or others in Iowa and Kentucky. The author tries to present obscure or unpublished texts, some with music.

8. Boswell, George W. "Folksongs in Northeastern Kentucky." *Kentucky Folklore Record* 11 (1965): 65-75.
A brief survey of songs collected in northeastern Kentucky by Boswell's students. An annotated list with county of collection and Child and Laws numbers. Gives two texts (no tunes), but refers to Child ballads, other English and American ballads, lyric folksongs, occupational songs, play-party songs, drinking songs, and religious folksongs.

9. ———. "Kentucky Folksongs in the Tennessee Archives." *Kentucky Folklore Record* 4 (1958): 115-21.
Around 1950 Boswell collected 48 songs from Nancy Priddy of Bonnieville. Describes the collection, which was recorded in Bowling Green. Gives texts and melodies with annotations. Focus is on ballads and native American folksongs.

10. ———. "Songs to Sing: 'There Was a Miller.'" *Kentucky Folklore Record* 4 (1958): 13-14.
The first in a series which ran from 1958 until 1976, each presenting a text with melody.

11. ———. "Songs to Sing: 'Burglar Man.'" *Kentucky Folklore Record* 14 (1968): 92-93.
A version from Johnson County.

12. ———. "A Song to Sing: 'The Mother-in-Law Song.'" *Kentucky Folklore Record* 15 (1969): 22-23.
A version collected by Boswell near Morehead.

13. ———. "A Song to Sing: 'Wild Bill Jones.'" *Kentucky Folklore Record* 15 (1969): 45.
A Knott County version collected by Taulbee Jacobs.

14. ———. "A Song to Sing: 'There Was an Old Lady.'" *Kentucky Folklore Record* 15 (1969): 66-67.
A Morgan County version of Child 10.

15. ———. "A Song to Sing: 'The Short Life of Trouble.'" *Kentucky Folklore Record* 17 (1971): 39-40.
Collected in Offut by Danny Daniels.

16. ———. "A Song to Sing: 'Molly Rand.'" *Kentucky Folklore Record* 17 (1971): 61-62.
A Morgan County version collected in 1964.

17. ———. "A Song to Sing." *Kentucky Folklore Record* 17 (1971): 83-84.

Text and music for a version of "One Morning in May" (Laws P14) from a Morgan County singer.

18. ———. "A Song to Sing: 'Lovin' Henry.'" *Kentucky Folklore Record* 18 (1972): 13-14.

A Morgan County version of Child 68.

19. ———. "A Song to Sing." *Kentucky Folklore Record* 18 (1972): 41-43.

A version of "The Demon Lover" (Child 243), presumably from Kentucky.

20. ———. "A Song to Sing: 'There Was a Rich Old Farmer.'" *Kentucky Folklore Record* 18 (1972): 75-76.

A Morgan County version.

21. ———. "A Song to Sing: 'Storms on the Sea.'" *Kentucky Folklore Record* 19 (1973): 15-16.

No annotation provided.

22. ———. "A Song to Sing: 'Pretty Polly.'" *Kentucky Folklore Record* 19 (1973): 87-88.

One text with two melodies.

23. ———. "A Song to Sing: 'Rose Mary and Tide.'" *Kentucky Folklore Record* 19 (1973): 117-18.

From Rowan County.

24. ———. "A Song to Sing: 'Mary and Willie.'" *Kentucky Folklore Record* 20 (1974): 111-12.

A version of Laws N28 from Todd County.

25. ———. "A Song to Sing: 'When I Was a Young Lad.'" *Kentucky Folklore Record* 21 (1975): 85-86.

A Christian County version of Laws E17.

26. ———. "A Song to Sing: 'William Hall.'" *Kentucky Folklore Record* 22 (1976): 52-53.

A Cub Run version of Laws N30 collected in 1950.

27. ———. "A Song to Sing: 'Nightingale.'" *Kentucky Folklore Record* 22 (1976): 77-78.

Laws P14, collected in 1950 in Cub Run.

28. ———. "A Song to Sing: 'Tibby Fowler.'" *Kentucky Folklore Record* 22 (1976): 100-101.

Song text; no annotation provided.

29. ———. "A Tale and Two Songs." *Kentucky Folklore Record* 9 (1963): 51-56.

Presents two native American ballads, texts and tunes, collected by a student from a male singer in Greenup County. Also includes a transcription, in stereotypical mountain dialect, of a folk narrative from the same informant.

30. Botkin, Benjamin. *A Treasury of Southern Folklore*. New York: Crown Publishers, 1949.
    A popular anthology containing eight song texts associated with Kentucky or with Kentucky singers. Also makes brief mention of the spiritual's origin at Kentucky camp meetings. Includes melodies; some texts are edited.
31. Bresler, Elya. "'Half Horse, Half Alligator' or 'Unfortunate Miss Baily and the Hunters of Kentucky.'" *Mountain Review* 2, no. 4 (1976): 10-11.
    Presents text and melody for a song the author believes to be one of the first original songs to come from Appalachia.
32. Brockway, Howard. *Nightingale*. New York: Gray, 1925.
    A song collected in Harlan County by Loraine Wyman, arranged for male quartet and piano accompaniment.
33. Burt, Olive Wooley. *American Murder Ballads and Their Stories*. New York: Citadel Press, 1964.
    Deals with the folklore of murder and songs based on actual killings. Several songs about Kentucky murders. Includes texts and melodies.
34. Calhoun, Cecil Warner. "Selected Instrumental Folk Music of South Central Kentucky." M.A. thesis, Iowa State University, 1941.
    A study by a native of the region who collected from friends and family. Includes 53 tunes.
35. Campbell, Marie. "Adam." *Kentucky Folklore Record* 8 (1962): 136.
    Words to one untitled song collected in Letcher County.
36. ———. "Answering-Back Song Ballads." *Tennessee Folklore Society Bulletin* 24, no. 1 (1958): 3-10.
    Three songs which pose questions, collected in the 1930s by the author, who taught in Gander (now Carcassone). Texts only; no melodies.
37. ———. "Cindy Give Out a Singing to Her House." *Tennessee Folklore Society Bulletin* 4, no. 4 (1937): 76-96.
    Written as if it were a short story. Presents a set of songs in a family context. Includes texts, melodies, and notes on informants. Derived from the author's work housed at Peabody College, Nashville.
38. ———. "Survivals of Old Folk Drama in the Kentucky Mountains." *Journal of American Folklore* 51 (1938): 10-24.
    Presents remnants of three plays formerly performed annually in the southern mountains. Includes five song texts associated

with the plays—three versions of Child 54 and two other songs. Collected in Gander (now Carcassone). Brief notes about informants.

39. Campbell, Olive Dame, and Cecil J. Sharp. *English Folk Songs from the Southern Appalachians*. New York: G.P. Putnam's Sons, 1917.
    The first edition of a major collection that includes considerable material from eastern Kentucky. Contains 323 variants of 122 songs collected in 1916 by Sharp, along with 32 songs in 42 variants collected ca. 1907-1910 by Campbell. Presents a wide range of genres. [For an expanded version edited by Maud Karpeles and published in 1932, see #182.]

40. Carmer, Carl. *America Sings: Stories and Songs of Our Nation's Growing*. New York: Alfred A. Knopf, 1942.
    A collection of songs and narratives for children. Includes a version of "Cumberland Gap."

41. ———, and Albert Sirmay. *Songs of the Rivers of America*. New York: Farrar and Rinehart, 1942.
    A songbook with piano arrangements. Includes three texts concerning the Kentucky River.

42. Carr, Mary. "'Poor Ellen Smith.'" *Kentucky Folk-Lore and Poetry Magazine* 3, no. 2 (1928): 21.
    Three verses of the song "Poor Ellen Smith" from the singing of Mary Carr. No musical notation.

43. Chase, Richard. *American Folk Tales and Songs: And Other Examples of English American Tradition as Preserved in the Appalachian Mountains and Elsewhere in the United States*. 1956. Reprint. New York: Dover, 1971.
    A collection that includes references to Pine Mountain as the source for some of the songs. With shape-notes and guitar chords.

44. ———. "The Seven Joys of Mary." *Mountain Life and Work* 33, no. 4 (1957): 23.
    A text of the English carol adapted from a Christmas card published by Pine Mountain Settlement School. Tune collected by Chase. No other information supplied.

45. ———, and Dorothy Nace, eds. *"A Year of Song": Pine Mountain Calendar, 1952*. Pine Mountain, Ky.: Pine Mountain Settlement School, 1952.
    Twelve folksongs from the southern mountains with texts and tunes. One is reprinted from *The Ballad Tree* by Evelyn Wells,

and two are from *Grandfather Tales* by Chase. No information given on the sources of the others.

46. "Cherry Tree, The." *Golden Book* 14 (December 1931): 395.
Presents "A Kentucky mountain ballad written down by R.W. Gordon." No melody.

47. Childs, Alice May. "Some Ballads and Folk-Songs from the South." M.A. thesis, University of Missouri, 1929.
"It is from the domestic tradition of the families of the upper grade of mountain society that almost all of my ballad texts come." Thirty-eight songs, largely from eastern Kentucky.

48. "Cindy." *Promenade* 5, no. 5-7 (November 1946): 3-4.
Melody and words collected by Margot Mayo from Rufus Crisp a native of Allen.

49. Clarke, David. *A Hymnbook: Containing a Copious Selection of Hymns and Spiritual Songs . . . Adapted to Tunes Commonly Used in Kentucky.* Harrodsburg: H. Miller, 1825.
A collection of religious songs contains little in the way of background or explanation of sources.

50. Cobb, Alice. "A Store of Song Ballads." *Mountain Life and Work* 22, no. 2 (1946): 3-5.
Primarily a revision of the author's 1935 article in *Notes from Pine Mountain Settlement School* [see #308] with texts.

51. Combs, Josiah H., ed. *All That's Kentucky: An Anthology.* Louisville: John P. Morton and Co., 1915.
A collection of songs, toasts, poems, short articles, and excerpts dealing with Kentucky.

52. ———. "'The Death of Sammie Adams.'" *Kentucky Folklore Record* 6, no. 4 (1960): 123-24.
The text of a local murder ballad collected in 1931 from A.B. Combs of Prestonsburg. No melody.

53. ———. *Folk-Songs from the Kentucky Highlands.* Schirmer's American Folk-Song Series, Set 1. New York: G. Schirmer, 1939.
A songbook of sixteen texts arranged for piano. Songs are "almost entirely from the southeastern part of Kentucky, largely from Knott County, in the heart of the 'pure feud belt.'" Some come from the author's mother; all are from his private collection.

54. ———. "A Traditional Ballad from the Kentucky Mountains." *Appalachian Heritage* 2, no. 4 (1974-1975): 58-59.
Gives text to a version of "Sweet William" from Hindman. No music.

55. ———. "A Traditional Ballad from the Kentucky Mountains." *Journal of American Folklore* 23 (1910): 381-82.
A version of "Fair Margaret and Sweet William" (Child 54) from Hindman. No music.

56. Cox, John Harrington. *Folk-Songs of the South*. 1925. Reprint. Hatboro, Pa.: Folklore Associates, 1963.
A major folksong collection, mainly ballads. Drawn primarily from West Virginia but includes a number of Kentucky informants. Specimen tunes in appendix.

57. "Cripple Creek." *Promenade* 1, no. 10 (n.d.): 5.
A square dance tune with words collected in Floyd County by Margot Mayo.

58. Daviess, Maria T. *History of Mercer and Boyle Counties*. Harrodsburg, Ky.: Harrodsburg Herald, 1924.
Reportedly contains a reference (p. 82) to "Lord Lovell." Copy not available for verification of citation or annotation.

59. Davisson, Ananias. *Kentucky Harmony, or A Choice Collection of Psalms, Tunes, Hymns, and Anthems*. 1816. Reprint. Minneapolis: Augsburg Publishing House, 1976.
A religious songbook with shape-notes. Author was a musician and printer born in Virginia in 1780. Songs were composed by the author in some cases, in other cases came from "gentlemen teachers from Virginia, Tennessee, and Kentucky" as well as from other printed sources.

60. Dickens, Hazel. "Black Lung." *Mountain Life and Work* 47, no. 4 (1971): 12-13.
A song composed by the author from the viewpoint of a Kentucky coal miner suffering from black lung.

61. Dreiser, Theodore. *Harlan Miners Speak: Report on Terrorism in the Kentucky Coalfields*. New York: Harcourt, Brace and Co., 1932.
Includes the text to Aunt Molly Jackson's "Kentucky Miners' Wives Ragged Hungry Blues."

62. Ellison, Catherine. "A Folk Song from Kentucky." *Western Folklore* 21 (1962): 110-13.
One children's song collected in Colorado from a woman who learned it from her Kentucky grandmother. Gives eight stanzas with music; refers to other published versions.

63. Federal Music Project. *Folk Songs from East Kentucky Collected by Folk Song Project of the Federal Music Project in Kentucky*. n.p. [Washington?]: Works Project Administration, 1939.

A mimeographed collection of texts, no melodies, with neither annotation nor introduction.

64. Ferrell, May Saunders. "'Composition and Song on the Death of Lottie Yates,' by Elijah Adams." *Kentucky Folklore Record* 21 (1975): 87-90.
A text copied from a broadside, probably of the 1870s or 1880s, of a murder ballad. Although the murder took place in Kentucky, this version was contributed by a woman from West Virginia.

65. "Folk Hymns for Singing: 'All Is Well.'" *Mountain Life and Work* 29, no. 2 (1953): 32.
Text and music for a white spiritual from the mountains.

66. "Folk Hymns for Singing: 'Evening Shade.'" *Mountain Life and Work* 29, no. 3 (1953): 20-21.
A mountain spiritual, with melody, associated with Pine Mountain Settlement School, Harlan County.

67. "Folk Hymns for Singing: 'Joseph and the Angel.'" *Mountain Life and Work* 29, no. 4 (1953): 24-25.
A white spiritual from the vicinity of Pine Mountain Settlement School. Includes melody.

68. "Folk Hymns for Singing: 'Wonderous Love.'" *Mountain Life and Work* 30, no. 2 (1954): 7.
An edited version of a white spiritual, with melody.

69. "Folk Songs for Singing: 'Aunt Sal's Song.'" *Mountain Life and Work* 27, no. 4 (1951): 42.
A song text printed as part of a Pine Mountain Settlement School calendar.

70. Foner, Philip Sheldon. *American Labor Songs of the Nineteenth Century.* Urbana: University of Illinois Press, 1975.
Contains two songs from eastern Kentucky as part of a significant anthology.

71. Ford, Ira W. *Traditional Music of America.* Hatboro, Pa.: Folklore Associates, 1965.
The author is a descendant of Kentuckians and learned some pieces from family tradition. The lack of annotations makes it impossible to ascertain whether the book contains Kentucky material. Primarily fiddle tunes.

72. Foster, Stephen Collins. *Forty Stephen Foster Songs.* Chicago: Hall and McCreary Co., 1934.
A songbook of 40 pieces by the author of "My Old Kentucky Home." Contains brief biographical information.

73. Fowke, Edith, and Joe Glazer. *Songs of Work and Protest.* New York: Dover Publications, 1973.

Originally published as *Songs of Work and Freedom* (Chicago: Roosevelt University, Labor Education Division, 1960), a songbook for social struggle which includes a number of Kentucky songs primarily concerning coal mining.

74. Franke, Margaret Allen. *Rhythmic Play-Songs*. Berea, Ky.: Berea College, 1954.

Eight singing games of doubtful traditional provenience.

75. Fuson, Henry Harvey. *Ballads of the Kentucky Mountains*. London: Mitre Press, 1931.

A wide-ranging collection of songs, including ballads, lyric folksongs, "jigs, play songs, nursery rhymes, war songs, and old religious songs." Texts only; no melodies. Written from Harlan.

76. ———. *Just from Kentucky: A Second Volume of Verse*. Louisville: John P. Morton and Co., 1925.

Poetry, some in heavy dialect, written by a Kentucky folksong collector and scholar.

77. Garland, Jim. "'I Don't Want Your Millions, Mister.'" *Mountain Life and Work* 47, no. 1 (1971): 18.

Presents the text for a protest song "written in 1932 during the dark days of the coal mining wars in Harlan County, Kentucky." Garland, a coal miner blacklisted for union organizing, was the younger brother of Aunt Molly Jackson.

78. Giles, Janice Holt. *40 Acres and No Mule*. Boston: Houghton Mifflin Co., 1967.

An autobiographical novel of life in southern Appalachia. Includes one religious song text and references to ballads and shape-note singing.

79. Glass, Paul, and Louis C. Singer. *Songs of Hill and Mountain Folk*. New York: Grosset and Dunlap, 1967.

Presents songs for singing from the highlands of Kentucky, Georgia, Alabama, the Carolinas, Tennessee, Virginia, and West Virginia. No significant annotation.

80. Greenway, John. *American Folksongs of Protest*. Phildelphia: University of Pennsylvania Press, 1953.

Argues that protest songs should be considered folksong even if the author is known; that authorship is unimportant is the significant fact. Presents a diverse collection of songs, including Kentucky materials.

81. Gregory, Yvonne. "Songs to Sing: 'Young John Riley.'" *Kentucky Folklore Record* 5 (1959): 137-38.

The text and tune of a version of Laws N37, collected in Elkton.

82. Grissom, Mary Allen. *The Negro Sings a New Heaven.* New York: Dover Publications, 1969.
Presents Afro-American sacred songs. "Most of the songs in this volume have been taken directly from the Negroes in their present-day worship, and have been selected from those sung in the neighborhood of Louisville, Kentucky, and certain rural sections in Adair County." Written in 1930. Includes melodies.

83. Hall, Eliza Calvert. *The Land of Long Ago.* Boston: Little, Brown, 1909.
A novel of life in the rural districts of the Pennyrile. Largely concerns genteel culture; includes two fragments of religious songs.

84. Harbison, David. "A Study in the Song Tradition of Metcalfe County, Kentucky." M.M. thesis, Southern Illinois University, 1971.
Approximately 250 texts, with melodies, collected by the author in small communities in a south-central Kentucky county. Includes brief background notes on the communities, the singers, and the region.

85. Harbison, Katherine. "In the Great Meadows and the Lone Prairie." *Southern Folklore Quarterly* 2 (1938): 149-56.
Texts and melodies for four Kentucky songs.

86. Hatcher, Mildred. "Folk Songs My Mother Sang." *Kentucky Folklore Record* 17 (1971): 78-82.
Presents four sentimental ballads learned in Murray. Some musical transcription.

87. Hatton, Sallie Lyttle. "Who Killed the Robin?" *Kentucky Folk-Lore and Poetry Magazine* 3, no. 2 (1928): 18.
Song text; no melody.

88. Helton, Roy. "'Old Christmas Morning': A Kentucky Mountain Ballad." *Appalachian Heritage* 6, no. 4 (1978): 6-7.
Gives text for a song claimed to be exclusively a Kentucky ballad. No melody.

89. Henry, Mellinger Edward. "Ballads and Songs of the Southern Highlands." *Journal of American Folklore* 42 (1929): 254-300.
A collection of songs from Kentucky and the rest of the southern highlands. Includes comparative headnotes and sample melodies.

90. ———. *Folk-Songs from the Southern Highlands.* New York: J.J. Augustin, 1938.
A collection of songs which includes Kentucky materials. Has extensive headnotes and many tunes. Most were collected by the author.

91. ———. "More Songs from the Southern Highlands." *Journal of American Folklore* 44 (1931): 61-115.
Three songs and variants collected in Kentucky, later reprinted in the author's *Songs Sung in the Southern Appalachians.* [See #92.]

92. ———. *Songs Sung in the Southern Appalachians.* London: Mitre Press, 1934.
A collection of song texts from the southern highlands, including Kentucky material. The introduction concerns the author's fieldwork. No melodies.

93. ———. "Still More Ballads and Folk-Songs from the Southern Highlands." *Journal of American Folklore* 45 (1932): 1-176.
A collection of songs with some melodies, including one piece from Kentucky, "The Cherry Tree Carol." Extensive headnotes.

94. "'Hills Shall Be Free, The.'" *Mountain Life and Work* 50, no. 1 (1974): 24.
The text of a song about coal mining in Kentucky. No music.

95. Holzknect, K.J. "Some Negro Song Variants from Louisville." *Journal of American Folklore* 41 (1928): 558-78.
Presents 30 religious songs and 15 secular pieces "obtained from a class of teachers in negro schools of Louisville, Kentucky." With annotations; no melodies.

96. "Hurry Liza Hurry." *Kentucky Folk-Lore and Poetry Magazine* 3, no. 2 (1928): 22-23.
One song text; no tune.

97. "I am a Pilgrim." *Sing Out!* 9, no. 3 (1959): 11.
The text and melody of a song popularized by Merle Travis.

98. "J.A. Steen Reminisces of Songs Heard in Childhood." *Glasgow* [Ky.] *Republican,* 19 January 1961, sec. 2, p. 1.
Three texts, words only, of humorous local songs composed by Dunk Murphy in the vicinity of the Fountain Run and Tracy communities.

99. Jackson, Aunt Molly. "The Hungry Blues." *New Masses,* December 1931, p. 4.
Text, words only, for a mining protest song written by Jackson.

100. Jackson, George Pullen. *Down-east Spirituals and Others: Three Hundred Songs Supplementary to the Author's Spiritual Folksongs of Early America.* New York: J.J. Augustin, 1939.
A collection of religious songs. Includes songs from the Shaker colony at South Union and references to Kentucky variants of some of the other songs in the anthology.

101. ———. *Spiritual Folk Songs of Early America: Two Hundred and Fifty Tunes and Texts with an Introduction and Notes.* New York: J.J. Augustin, 1937.
A collection of songs drawn from several singing books and hymnals. Includes text and tune with data on origins and other versions. Not enough information to determine the extent of Kentucky material.

102. Jameson, Gladys V. "Hymn of Praise." *Mountain Life and Work* 32, no. 2 (1956): 38.
A hymn published in Louisville in 1850. With melody.

103. ———. "Mountain Ballads." *Mountain Life and Work* 1, no. 3 (1925): 12, 19.
A text, with melody, for "Paper of Pins," and general remarks on ballads.

104. ———. "Music Section: 'The Cuckoo.'" *Mountain Life and Work* 2, no. 4 (1927): 32.
A Knott County song text with melody.

105. ———. *Sweet River of Song: Authentic Ballads, Hymns, Folksongs from the Appalachian Region.* Berea, Ky.: Berea College, 1967.
A small collection of 57 hymns, ballads, lyric folksongs, fiddle tunes, singing games, and children's songs. Text and tune are provided for each song along with a brief explanatory note.

106. ———. *Wake and Sing.* New York: Associated Music Publishers, 1955.
"A miniature anthology of the music of Appalachian America." More than half is sacred music; also contains ballads and fiddle tunes. Texts are with music.

107. Jewell, James William. *Kentucky Mountain Melodies.* Lexington: Lang Co., 1950.
A collection of approximately 170 songs with arranged melodies from the repertoire of the author's family and the Carrol family. The very varied selection includes songs of doubtful traditionality. No notes other than a brief introduction.

108. Jones, Blanche Preston. "England Still Lives in the Kentucky Hills." *Arcadian Life* 53 (Spring 1942): 40-41.
Notes on the author's visit to a Lawrence County school where kinship with Britain is strongly felt. Includes references to the singing of Anglo-American songs, and the text, words only, of the author's ballad about Winston Churchill.

109. Kincaid, Bradley. *My Favorite Mountain Ballads and Old-Time Songs.* Books 1, 2, and 3. Chicago: Prairie Farmer Radio

Station, 1928.
Songbooks by a popular radio singer from Kentucky that
include many traditional songs.

110. Kittredge, George L., ed. "Ballads and Rhymes from Kentucky." *Journal of American Folklore* 20 (1907): 251-77.
Presents texts for five Child ballads, twelve other ballads, and
six children's songs originally collected by Katherine Pettit of
Hindman. The author supplies annotations.

111. ———, ed. "Ballads and Songs." *Journal of American Folklore*
30 (1917): 283-369.
Presents texts and tunes from various collectors, including
sixteen from Kentucky contributed by Loraine Wyman. Notes
give name of informant and references to other published
versions.

112. Korson, George. *Coal Dust on the Fiddle*. 1943. Reprint.
Hatboro, Pa.: Folklore Associates, 1965.
Songs presented in the context of coal miners' lives. Includes
Kentucky materials but also covers Pennsylvania, Ohio, Illi-
nois, Indiana, Virginia, West Virginia, Tennessee, and Ala-
bama. Most texts are without melodies.

113. Krehbiel, Henry Edward. *Afro-American Folksongs: A Study
in Racial and National Music*. New York: G. Schirmer, 1914.
A classic study that includes a number of songs—spirituals,
shouts, and others—from Kentucky, primarily Boyle County.

114. Lawson, Elizabeth. "'I Am on My Way.'" *Kentucky Folk-Lore
and Poetry Magazine* 3, no. 2 (1928): 20.
A religious song text; no melody.

115. Leonard, Silas White, and A.D. Fillmore. *The Christian
Psalmist, A Collection of Hymns and Tunes of Various
Metres—Original and Selected: Embracing the Round Note,
the Numeral, and the Patent Note Systems of Notation*.
Louisville, Ky.: S.W. Leonard, 1848.
Texts and tunes to a large number of nineteenth-century
hymns popular in Kentucky.

116. "Let's Play Josie." *Kentucky Folk-Lore and Poetry Magazine* 3,
no. 2 (1928): 21-22.
A song text; no music. The article may have been written by
Mary Carr.

117. Lomax, Alan. *Folk Songs of North America*. Garden City, N.Y.:
Doubleday and Co., 1960.
Contains Kentucky texts, words and melodies, for a variety of
genres.

118. ———, Woody Guthrie, and Pete Seeger. *Hard Hitting Songs for Hard-Hit People*. New York: Oak Publications, 1967.

A collection of songs from the Depression years. Includes a section called "Hell Busts Loose in Kentucky," containing several coal-mining and union songs written by Aunt Molly Jackson, Sarah Ogan Gunning, Jim Garland, and others. Text and tune provided for each song.

119. Lomax, John A., and Alan Lomax. *American Ballads and Folk Songs*. New York: Macmillan Co., 1967.

A collection of texts and tunes, some combined from various sources or taken from other collections. Several tunes supplied by James Howard, a blind fiddler from Harlan. Some stanzas taken from Jean Thomas, Josiah Combs, and other Kentucky collectors.

120. ———. *Our Singing Country*. New York: Macmillan Co., 1941.

About 35 of the approximately 200 songs are from Kentucky. Frequent references to Hazard.

121. McGill, Josephine. "The Cherry Tree Carol." *Journal of American Folklore* 29 (1916): 293-94.

Presents nine stanzas (text only) of an American version of the British ballad (Child 54) found by McGill in Knott County. She believes it is the first published appearance of this particular ballad in America.

122. ———. *Folk Songs of the Kentucky Mountains*. New York: Boosey and Co., 1917, 1926.

One of the earliest collecions of Kentucky folksongs, collected in Knott and Letcher counties in 1914. Child numbers are noted. Includes texts and piano arrangements. Introduction by Henry E. Krehbiel.

123. Metcalf, Samuel L. *Kentucky Harmonist*. Cincinnati: The author, 1820.

A shape-note hymnal.

124. Miller, Doris C. "'Blue Jacket and Trousers.'" *Kentucky Folklore Record* 16 (1970): 11-14.

A song text arranged for piano and voice. Includes what is apparently a family narrative connecting the song to a family member's return home from the Civil War.

125. Montell, William Lynwood, ed., *Monroe County Folklife*. Bowling Green, Ky.: The author, 1975.

Includes texts (no tunes) of 37 folksongs collected from informants in Monroe County. Notes identify informants and key the texts to scholarly indexes of Child and Laws as well as other regional folksong collections.

126. ———. *Monroe County History, 1820-1970*. Tompkinsville, Ky.: Tompkinsville Lions Club, 1970.
Contains the remnant of an Afro-American roustabout song about the steamboat *Benton McMillan* as well as the text of a composed ballad about the "Tompkinsville Tornado."

127. Moore, Arthur K. "Neighbors: Kentucky: A Metrical Version of 'The Wonderful Hunt.'" *New York Folklore Quarterly* 7 (1951): 236-40.
A song version, with melody, from a Russellville informant. The text is related to a common folk narrative motif.

128. ———. "Types of the Folk Song 'Father Grumble.'" *Journal of American Folklore* 64 (1951): 89-94.
Includes one stanza, with melody, of a song learned from a great-grandmother from Kentucky.

129. Moses, P.J. "'Old Yellow's Dead.'" *Kentucky Folk-Lore and Poetry Magazine* 3, no. 2 (1928): 19.
One song text, without melody, probably from Kentucky.

130. ———. "'The Sons of Levi.'" *Kentucky Folk-Lore and Poetry Magazine* 3, no. 2 (1928): 20.
One song text, probably from Kentucky. No melody.

131. "Music Section." *Mountain Life and Work* 2, no. 2 (1926): 47.
A text, with melody, for "Down in the Valley" as sung by Lula Hale of Quicksand.

132. Niles, John Jacob. *The Ballad Book of John Jacob Niles*. Boston: Houghton Mifflin Co., 1961.
Presents texts with music for a number of ballads collected by the author. Includes brief headnotes and a biographical introduction.

133. ———. *Ballads, Carols and Tragic Legends*. New York: G. Schirmer, 1937.
Ten songs with accompaniment.

134. ———. *Ballads, Carols and Tragic Legends from the Southern Appalachian Mountains*. New York: G. Schirmer, 1937.
"Collected and simply arranged with piano accompaniment" by Niles.

135. ———. *Ballads, Love-Songs, and Tragic Legends from the Southern Appalachian Mountains*. New York: G. Schirmer, 1938.
A songbook of texts collected and arranged for piano by Niles.

136. ———. *More Songs of the Hill-Folk*. New York: G. Schirmer, 1936.
   A songboook subtitled "Ten Ballads and Tragic Legends from Kentucky, Virginia, Tennessee, North Carolina, and Georgia." Arranged for voice and piano.

137. ———. *Seven Kentucky Mountain Songs*. New York: G. Schirmer, 1928.
   A songbook compiled by the singer-collector.

138. ———. *Seven Negro Exaltations*. New York: G. Shirmer, [ca. 1929].
   A singing book.

139. ———. *Songs of the Hill-Folk*. New York: G. Shirmer, n.d.
   Twelve songs collected and arranged for piano by Niles. Includes texts from eastern Kentucky.

140. ———. *Ten Christmas Carols from the Southern Appalachian Mountains*. New York: G. Schirmer, 1935.
   A songbook arranged for voice and piano. Incudes four texts from Kentucky.

141. ———. *The Anglo-American Ballad Study Book Containing Eight Ballads in Current Tradition in the United States of America*. New York: G. Schirmer, 1945.
   Texts and music arranged by the author. Includes four Child ballads.

142. ———. *The Anglo-American Carol Study Book Containing English Carols in the Early Traditional Form and Surviving Versions Traditional in the United States*. New York: G. Schirmer, 1948.
   A songbook with Niles's arrangements.

143. ———. "Two Songs." *Phonews*, Winter 1964, 11-14.
   Two song texts with melodies. Also includes a bibliography of the author's publications.

144. "'O My Love and Turn Again.'" *Kentucky Folk-Lore and Poetry Magazine* 3, no. 2 (1928): 23-24.
   A song text, perhaps from Kentucky. No melody.

145. Owens, Bess A. "Some Unpublished Folk-Songs of the Cumberlands," M.A. thesis, Peabody College, 1930.
   "This is a collection of some unpublished folksongs heard today in the mountains of Eastern Kentucky. The purpose of the study is to present in a standard and readable form, without emendations, the texts of the ballads and songs according to the themes treated, and to retrace, as far as possible, their origin and manner of tramsmission." Contains 157 songs from Pike County.

146. ——. "Songs of the Cumberlands." *Journal of American Folklore* 49 (1936): 215-42.

A presentation of 24 songs, both ballads and lyric folksongs, all with melodies. Many come from students in Pikeville.

147. Oxrieder, Julia. "Heeple Steeple or London Bridge." *Kentucky Folklore Record* 21 (1975): 105-18.

Includes a fragment of song text collected in Kentucky in 1912 based on the common children's counting-out rhyme.

148. Perrow, E.C. "Songs and Rhymes from the South." *Journal of American Folklore* 25 (1912): 137-55.

Contains an eastern Kentucky version of "Jesse James."

149. ——. "Songs and Rhymes from the South." *Journal of American Folklore* 26 (1913): 123-73.

A number of Kentucky texts, some with musical notation, in a variety of genres.

150. ——. "Songs and Rhymes from the South." *Journal of American Folklore* 28 (1915): 129-90.

A number of Kentucky texts.

151. Pine Mountain Settlement School. "Folk Songs for Singing: 'Lolly-too-dum.'" *Mountain Life and Work* 27, no. 3 (1951): 38-39.

A song, with melody, collected in the vicinity of the settlement school.

152. ——. *Song Ballads and Other Songs of the Pine Mountain Settlement School.* Harlan County, Ky.: Pine Mountain Settlement School, 1923.

A book of songs sung at the settlement school, texts only. Songs from Kentucky, the Appalachian region, England, and elsewhere.

153. Pound, Louise. "American Text of 'Robin Hood and Little John.'" *American Speech* 2 (1927): 75.

A song text from a Nebraska informant who learned it from her grandmother, who had learned it in Kentucky. No melody.

154. "Prettiest Little Baby in the Country-O." *Sing Out!* 9, no. 4 (1960): 7.

Text and music of a children's song from the repertoire of Jean Ritchie.

155. Raines, Clarinda. "'Billy and Diana.'" *Kentucky Folk-Lore and Poetry Magazine* 3, no. 2 (1928): 18.

A song text, no melody, probably from Kentucky.

156. Reece, Florence. "Which Side Are You On?" *Mountain Life and Work* 49, no. 10 (1973): 5.

An organizing song from the Kentucky coalfields. No melody.

157. ———, and Guy Carawan. "'The Strike': A Song and a Prayer for the End of Stearns Troubles." *Mountain Life and Work* 53, no. 11 (1977): 24-25.
A song from the 1976 Blue Diamond Company strike. Includes melody.

158. Richardson, Ethel Park, comp. *American Mountain Songs.* New York: Greenberg, 1927.
Songs from the mountains of Tennessee, the Carolinas, north Georgia, Kentucky, Virginia, and Missouri divided into ballads, lonesome and love tunes, spirituals, and nonsense songs. No information on provenience of specific texts. Melodies arranged by Sigmund Spaeth.

159. Ritchie, Edna [Edna Ritchie Baker]. "Folk Songs for Singing: 'Pretty Little Pink.'" *Mountain Life and Work* 26, no. 3 (1950): 13-14.
A song text, with melody, learned by a member of the famous singing family when she taught school at Lotts Creek, Cordia.

160. Ritchie, Jean. *A Garland of Mountain Song.* New York: Broadcast Music, 1953.
Songs for singing from the repertoire of the celebrated Ritchie family. Notes give the family context. The forward by Alan Lomax discusses the family, concentrating on Jean.

161. ———. "'Black Waters.'" *Appalachian Heritage* 1, no. 3 (1973): 52-54.
A review of the singer's album *Celebration of Life.* Includes text, with melody, of a song composed by Ritchie.

162. ———. *Celebration of Life.* New York: Geordie Music Publishing, 1971.
Songs and poetry from Jean Ritchie. Many of the songs are composed or arranged by the author. With melodies and guitar chords.

163. ———. *Folk Songs of the Southern Appalachians as Sung by Jean Ritchie.* New York: Oak Publications, 1965.
An illustrated songbook presenting songs from the Perry County native's repertoire. Alan Lomax's foreword includes a biography of the singer. Nicely illustrated with photographs.

164. ———. *Jean Ritchie's Dulcimer People.* New York: Oak Publications, 1975.
A songbook with notes on dulcimer players and techniques.

165. ———. *Jean Ritchie's Swapping Song Book.* New York: H.Z. Walck, 1964.
A songbook targeted primarily at children. The foreword by Oscar Brand is biographical.

166. ———, ed. *The Newport Folk Festival Songbook*. New York: Alfred Music Co., 1965.

A selection of songs as sung at the festival in the early 1960s, including samples from the repertoires of a number of Kentucky musicians, such as Bill Monroe, Sarah Gunning, Jean and Edna Ritchie, and others.

167. ———. *The Swapping Song Book*. New York: Oxford University Press, 1952.

A songbook for children featuring 21 songs, each introduced by a full-page photograph together with a brief story of daily life in the Kentucky mountains. Arranged for piano.

168. Roberts, Leonard, ed. "Floyd County Folklore." *Kentucky Folklore Record* 2 (1956): 33-66.

The Floyd County native presents a selection of narratives, drama, games, rhymes, ballads, and other songs. Texts are annotated; no melodies.

169. ———. "Folk Songs for Singing: 'The Bachelor Boy.'" *Mountain Life and Work* 30, no. 2 (1954): 6.

A text with melody from the singing of Jim Couch of Harlan County.

170. ———, and C. Buell Agey. *In the Pine: Selected Kentucky Folksongs*. Pikeville, Ky.: Pikeville College Press, 1978.

One hundred and forty-three songs collected in 1947-1955 by Roberts and his students in eastern Kentucky. With headnotes. Musical transcriptions and analyses by Agey. Includes ballads, British and American; lyrics; sacred songs; sentimental pieces; and songs of humor and satire. Roberts provides notes on his experiences as a fieldworker in the mountains.

171. ———, and students. "Stella Kenney." *Kentucky Folklore Record* 8 (1962): 113-24.

A murder ballad collected by students, derived from a crime in Carter County. History, text, and melody.

172. "Rocky Hill." *Promenade* 8, no. 2 (November 1948): 4.

Words and melody collected by Margot Mayo from Rufus Crisp of Allen.

173. "The Rodeheaver Negro Spirituals." *Kentucky Folk-Lore and Poetry Magazine* 4, no. 3 (1929): 7-9.

Texts only for three spirituals.

174. Rohrbough, Lyn, ed. *Country Life Songs*. Delaware, Ohio: CRS, n.d.

Includes Kentucky songs recorded and arranged by Gladys Jameson, taken from *Lonesome Tunes* [see #241], and from the Ritchie family.

175. Russell, Esther. "The Dogwood Hymn." *Mountain Life and Work* 35, no. 1 (1959): 22-23.

A religious song, with melody, from Red Bird Mission.

176. Sandburg, Carl. *The American Songbag*. New York: Harcourt Brace Jovanovich, 1955.

About 35 of the 280 pieces in this songbook are linked to Kentucky. A variety of genres with "complete harmonizations" or piano arrangements.

177. Sanders, Myra. " 'Toady Went a Courting.' " *Kentucky Folk-Lore and Poetry Magazine* 3, no. 4 (1929): 12-13.

The text to a version of "Froggie Went a Courting."

178. Scarborough, Dorothy. *On the Trail of Negro Folk-Songs*. Cambridge: Harvard University Press, 1925.

A classic collection that includes several Kentucky references.

179. Schmitz, R.M. "Leo Frank and Mary Phagan." *Journal of American Folklore* 60 (1947): 59-61.

A version of a murder ballad collected in Lamb, Kentucky, concerning a crime in Atlanta. No melody.

180. Schott, Tom. *Sing Of America*. New York: Thomas Y. Crowell, 1947.

"It is impossible to recall when and where I learned many of the songs in this book. Some of them I must have been born with. . . . Some I have learned from my wife, who taught school in the Kentucky mountains." Thirty-five songs arranged by the author; sources generally not listed.

181. Segales, Virginia Jean. "Development of American Folk Music." M.A. thesis, College-Conservatory of Music of Cincinnati, 1947.

Includes a few musical examples from the Kentucky mountains.

182. Sharp, Cecil J. *English Folk Songs from the Southern Appalachians*. 2 vols. Ed. Maud Karpeles. London: Oxford University Press, 1932.

A landmark collection done in 1916-1918 by the noted English collector-scholar. Contains a wide variety of genres. Texts are given with music and variants. Over half the songs have at least one variant collected in eastern Kentucky. [*see also* #39.]

183. ———. *Folk-Songs of English Origins Collected in the Appalachian Mountains*. London: Novello and Co., n.d. [ca. 1918].

A songbook featuring 12 songs arranged for piano. Drawn from the author's field research.

184. ———. *Nursery Songs from the Appalachian Mountains*. 2nd series. London: Novello and Co., n.d. [ca. 1923].

Seventeen songs with piano arrangements. Not the same as the author's *Seventeen Nursery Songs from the Appalachian Mountains* [see #186].

185. ———. *Nursery Songs from the Appalachian Mountains.* 2 vols. London: Oxford University Press, 1932.
Children's songs aranged for piano.

186. ———. *Seventeen Nursery Songs from the Appalachian Mountains.* London: Novello and Co., n.d.
A songbook with piano arrangements.

187. ———, and Maud Karpeles. *Eighty English Folk Songs from the Southern Appalachians.* Cambridge, Mass.: MIT Press, 1968.
A songbook based on Sharp and Karpeles's earlier fieldwork. Includes a number of songs from Kentucky.

188. Sheets, Bill G. *America's Most Beloved Folk Ballads.* Lexington, Ky.: Bill G. Sheets, 1965.
A collection of traditional ballads, tragic, sentimental, humorous, and cowboy. Notes on each song provide a brief explanation, but no sources are listed. May be Kentucky songs. No melodies.

189. Shelby, Richard. "A Small Bag of Ballads from the Hills." *Appalachian Heritage* 1, no. 1 (1973): 31-36.
Three murder ballads with music—one local, one American, one Child—from eastern Kentucky.

190. Silber, Irwin, ed. *American Favorite Ballads: Tunes and Songs as Sung by Pete Seeger.* New York: Oak Publications, 1961.
A songbook with words and music to over 80 songs from Seeger's repertoire, including versions of "Cumberland Gap," "Darlin' Corey," and "Which Side Are You On?"

191. *Six Folk Songs from the Southern Highlands.* Recreation Service of the Conference of Southern Mountain Workers. Delaware, Ohio: CRS, 1938.
A booklet of songs from Tennessee, North Carolina, and Kentucky along with a group of chanteys and other songs collected by Cecil Sharp.

192. Skean, Marion. *Circle Left.* Ary, Ky.: Homeplace, 1939.
A variety of games from Breathitt, Perry, and Wolfe counties. Includes melodies and song texts as well as directions. The author asserts that she attempted to record the games exactly as she observed them.

193. Smith, John F. "Ballads and Folk Songs." *Kentucky Folk-Lore and Poetry Magazine* 2, no. 1 (1927): 8-16.

Eleven Kentucky song texts selected by Smith from various contributors. No musical notation is provided.

194. ———. "Ballads and Songs." *Kentucky Folk-Lore and Poetry Magazine* 1, no. 4 (1927): 12-14.

Texts for "I Will Sing You a Song" and "Darby's Sheep."

195. ———, ed. "Special Folk-Lore Number." *Kentucky Folk-Lore and Poetry Magazine* 2, no. 4 (1928): 1-26.

A special issue containing texts of 27 songs, of which 9 are associated with singing games. No musical notation or information on sources.

196. "Soldier's Joy." *Promenade* 1, no. 7 (n.d.): 4.

Words and melody collected by Margot Mayo from the playing of Rufus Crisp of Allen.

197. " 'Solidarity Forever.' " *Mountain Life and Work* 47, no. 2 (1971): 10.

The text of a union song. No melody.

198. "Songs." *Appalachian Heritage* 2, no. 1 (1974): 38-40.

Includes two stanzas of "Come All You Fair and Tender Ladies" from eastern Kentucky.

199. *Songs of All Time.* Delaware, Ohio: CRS, 1946.

A songbook published for the Council of Southern Mountain Workers. Includes pieces from the Ritchie family repertoire. [*See also* #200.]

200. *Songs of All Time.* Revised ed. Berea, Ky.: Council of the Southern Mountains, 1957.

A songbook featuring a number of texts from Kentucky, with melodies. Foreword signed by Edna Ritchie, Raymond K. McLain, Richard Chase, and Marie Marvel. [*See also* #199.]

201. "Songs of Richard Burnett, The." *Old Time Music* 10 (Autumn 1973): 10-11.

Four texts from a songbook entitled *Songs Sung by R.D. Burnett, The Blind Man, Monticello, Kentucky.*

202. "Songs to Sing: 'The Noble Young Squire (Dog and Gun).' " *Kentucky Folklore Record* 13 (1967): 68-70.

A version of Laws N20 collected from Uncle Lewis Jimison Bumgarner of New Haven. With melody.

203. "Sourwood Mountain." *Promenade* 1, no. 1 (n.d.): 4.

Words only to a Kentucky version (probably collected by Margot Mayo).

204. "Steel-driving John Henry." *Promenade* 2, no. 10 (December 1941): 5.

As sung by Rufus Crisp from Allen, as well as by a Tennessee singer (probably collected by Margot Mayo).

205. Stuart, Jesse. *The Thread that Runs So True*. Chicago: Dramatic Publishing Co., 1958.
The writer's autobiography includes two stanzas and explanation of a play-party song.
206. Sturgill, Virgil L. "The Murder of Lottie Yates." *Kentucky Folklore Record* 5 (1959): 61-64.
Text and music of a Carter County murder ballad collected in 1957.
207. ———. "The Murder of Lottie Yates." *North Carolina Folklore* 6, no. 2 (1958): 26-28.
A murder ballad from Carter County, with melody.
208. ———. "My Most Successful Collecting Experience." *Kentucky Folklore Record* 12 (1966): 4-5.
Refers to two Carter County murder ballads.
209. Sulzer, Elmer Griffith. *Twenty-Five Kentucky Folk Ballads*. Lexington, Ky.: Transylvania Printing Co., 1936.
A variety of genres (texts and music) collected by the author, who writes, "Words to the ballads are as complete as good taste permits."
210. *Sweet Freedom's Song*. Delaware, Ohio: CRS, n.d.
Includes a variety of songs from eastern Kentucky, some published previously elsewhere. A number of songs come from the singing of the Ritchie family; others were collected by Gladys Jameson.
211. "'Sweet Sixteen.'" *Kentucky Folk-Lore and Poetry Magazine* 3, no. 2 (1928): 24.
Seven stanzas and the chorus of the song "Sweet Sixteen." No musical notation or documentation of source.
212. Thomas, Jean [Jeannette Bell Thomas]. "The Art of Ballad Making in the Kentucky Mountains." *Kentucky School Journal* 16, no. 9 (May 1938): 29-32.
An overview of mountain singing with emphasis on local songs. Includes texts.
213. ———. "Ballads and Their Stories." *Letters* 5, no. 18 (February 1932): 14-21.
The noted festival organizer and champion of Kentucky grassroots music presents three song texts.
214. ———. *Big Sandy*. New York: Henry Holt and Co., 1940.
A portrait of life in an eastern Kentucky valley. Contains a number of texts (words only) and descriptions of singing and musical contexts. One chapter (pp. 286-96) on the "Singin' Gatherin'"—the American Folk Song Festival.

215. Thomas, Jeannette Bell [Jean], and Joseph A. Leeder. *The Singin' Gatherin': Tunes from the Southern Appalachians.* New York: Silver Burdette Co., 1939.
Primarily a songbook of texts collected by Thomas.

216. Treat, Asher E. "Kentucky Folksong in Northern Wisconsin." *Journal of American Folklore* 52 (1939): 1-51.
A variety of songs collected from Kentucky natives. Includes notes on informants and texts with melodies.

217. ———. "The Singing Kentucks Move West." In *Folklore of the Great West: Selections from Eighty-three Years of the Journal of American Folklore,* pp. 237-46. Ed. John Greenway. Palo Alto: American West Publishing Co., 1969.
Texts of several songs of Kentucky migrants in Wisconsin.

218. Truitt, Florence. "Songs from Kentucky." *Journal of American Folklore* 36 (1923): 376-79.
Four untitled humorous songs, including "The Darby Ram," collected by the author around the turn of the century. No notes.

219. "Wagoner's Lad, The." *Promenade* 8, no. 6 (April 1952): 3.
Words and melody collected from Lulu Crisp of Allen by Margot Mayo. Arranged for piano.

220. Walker, William. *The Southern Harmony Song Book.* 1847. Reprint. New York: Hastings House, 1939.
A shape-note hymnal with information on the Benton Big Singing.

221. Watson, Lindsey. *The Singer's Choice: A Collection of Tunes, Hymns and Anthems, Original and Selected, Designed for Church and School Purposes.* Louisville: J.P. Morton, 1854.
An early hymnal whose texts were "compiled, arranged and composed" by the author.

222. Wells, Evelyn K. "Songs from Pine Mountain." *Notes from Pine Mountain Settlement School* 7, no. 1 (1935).
An unpaginated publication that includes 10 texts, melodies, and notes on sources. From the eastern part of the state.

223. West, Don. *Songs for Southern Workers.* Huntington, W.Va.: Appalachian Movement Press, 1978.
Union organizing songs composed by the activist poet, set to familiar melodies.

224. Wheeler, Mary. *Steamboatin' Days.* Baton Rouge: Louisiana State University Press, 1944.
Songs, with melodies, collected from Afro-Americans working along the Ohio River.

225. "When I Can Read My Titles." *Promenade* 7, no. 1 (January 1948): 3.
     An Allen, Kentucky, version of a religious piece, collected by Margot Mayo. Includes melody.
226. White, Newman I. *American Negro Folk-Songs*. Cambridge, Mass.: Harvard University Press, 1928.
     Includes chapters on religious songs, dance songs, ballads, animal songs, work songs, and blues. Texts but no music. Source given; some songs are from Kentucky, but most are not.
227. Whitley, Mrs. W.H. "Adam and Eve." *Kentucky Folklore Record* 8 (1962): 59-60.
     The text of a song sung at a Marion County wedding in 1814. No melody.
228. Wilgus, D.K. "Addenda from the Josiah H. Combs Collection." *Kentucky Folklore Record* 7 (1961): 176.
     Eleven texts which supplement the Combs collection as duplicated for the Western Kentucky State College (now Western Kentucky University) folklore archive.
229. ———. "Down Our Way: Open the 'Ballet Box.'" *Kentucky Folklore Record* 1 (1955): 85-89.
     Four texts, no music, from "ballets" kept by a Butler County resident.
230. ———. "Folksongs of Kentucky, East and West." *Kentucky Folklore Record* 3 (1957): 89-118.
     Eighteen songs, most with music, from three unpublished sources: the archive at Western Kentucky State College, the Herbert Halpert Folklore Archive at Blackburn College, and a manuscript sent by Alice May Childs from Frenchburg.
231. ———. "Local Ballads: 'Arch and Gordon.'" *Kentucky Folklore Record* 6 (1960): 51-56.
     Two variants of a murder ballad based on a Louisville crime. Two texts, one melody.
232. Williams, Cratis D. "Local Ballads: 'Caines Creek Distillery.'" *Kentucky Folklore Record* 6 (1960): 91-92.
     A Lawrence County local song and its background. No melody.
233. ———. "Local Ballads: 'Jesse Adams.'" *Kentucky Folklore Record* 8 (1962): 19-20.
     A murder ballad associated with Lawrence County. No melody.
234. ———. "Local Ballads: 'John Ferguson.'" *Kentucky Folklore Record* 6 (1960): 15-20.
     A murder ballad from Lawrence County. No melody.

235. ———. "Local Ballads: 'John Kelley.'" *Kentucky Folklore Record* 7 (1961): 15-16.
A local song about a family that lived on Cherokee Creek, Lawrence County. No melody.

236. ———. "Local Ballads: 'Laura Belle.'" *Kentucky Folklore Record* 8 (1962): 53-54.
A ballad "rhymer" from Brushy Ford, Lawrence County. No tune.

237. ———. "'Lottie Yates.'" *Kentucky Folklore Record* 5 (1959): 65-69.
A murder ballad from a Lawrence County informant. No melody.

238. ———, and Alice May Childs. "Local Ballads: 'Stella Kenney.'" *Kentucky Folklore Record* 5 (1959): 131-35.
Two versions of a murder ballad, one from Lawrence County, one collected by a student at Pikeville College. No tune.

239. Willis, Robert. *The Lexington Cabinet and Repository of Sacred Music.* Cincinnati: J.A. James and Co., 1838.
A shape-note hymnal by a Lexington author.

240. Wilson, Jess D. *When They Hanged the Fiddler.* Berea, Ky.: Kentucke [sic] Imprints, 1978.
An anthology of the author's columns from the *Rural Kentuckian.* Has references to dancing and singing. Includes a number of texts.

241. Wyman, Loraine, and Howard Brockway. *Lonesome Tunes: Folk Songs from the Kentucky Mountains.* New York: H.W. Gray Co., 1916.
A historic collection by Wyman with piano arrangements by Brockway. Texts are from eastern Kentucky.

242. ———. *Twenty Kentucky Mountain Songs.* Boston: Oliver Ditson Co., 1920.
An early songbook arranged for voice and piano, containing texts collected by Wyman in eastern Kentucky.

243. "'Young Charlotte.'" *Kentucky Folk-Lore and Poetry Magazine* 3, no. 2 (1928): 25-26.
A nine-stanza text of the ballad "Young Charlotte." No musical notation. Information on the source not provided.

Fieldworkers, Collectors, and Scholars

Also see entries: #208, 228, 320, 338, 459, 540, 640, 649, 675, 680, 691, 692, 701

244. Bidstrup, Marguerite Butler. "Ballad Collector." *Mountain Life and Work* 30, no. 4 (1954): 23-29.
    Looks at Olive Dame Campbell's role as a collector and preserver of Appalachian folksongs and her association with Cecil Sharp. Includes text and tune to "Ole King Quine," a song collected by Campbell, reprinted from *Songs of All Time.*
245. Brockway, Howard. "The Quest of the Lonesome Tune." *Art World* 2 (1917): 227-30.
    A discussion of Brockway and Loraine Wyman's 1916 "expedition" to southeastern Kentucky for the purpose of collecting folksongs.
246. "Carpenteering Folk Songs." *Musical Courier* 80 (April 22, 1920): 22.
    A response to an article published elsewhere which claimed that white Americans have little in the way of folksong. Makes reference to Josephine McGill's fieldwork in eastern Kentucky.
247. "Cecil Sharp: He Reaped a Rich Harvest of Song." *Mountain Life and Work* 29, no. 4 (1953): 12-13.
    A brief summary of Sharp's work in America, based on information from *The Ballad Tree* by Evelyn Wells [see #490]. No texts.
248. Chandler, George Wallace, Jr. "The History and Present Status of Folk-Song Scholarship in the South." M.A. thesis, University of North Carolina, 1936.
    Claims that until 1914 Kentucky and Missouri were the two states in which the most song collection and scholarship occurred.
249. Clarke, Kenneth, and Mary Clarke. *The Harvest and the Reapers: Oral Traditions of Kentucky.* Lexington: University Press of Kentucky, 1974.
    A historical examination of the study of folklore in Kentucky,

published as part of the University Press of Kentucky's Bicentennial Bookshelf series. The chapter on folksong deals with songs, singers and their lives, and scholars of folksong. Includes two complete texts and a number of illustrative fragments; no musical transcriptions.

250. Cohen, John. "A Visitor's Recollections." *Southern Exposure* 5, no. 2-3 (1977): 115-18.

Cohen describes trips to eastern Kentucky in 1959 and 1961 during which he gathered material for the Folkways LP *Mountain Music of Kentucky* (Folkways FA 2317) and the film *High Lonesome Sound,* both featuring the music of Roscoe Holcomb.

251. ———. "Field Trip—Kentucky." *Sing Out!* 10, no. 2 (1960): 13-15.

Describes a 1959 field trip to Kentucky by Cohen, who is a filmmaker, photographer, and revivalist musician. Mentions a variety of genres, including lining out, shape-note singing, "hootenanny styled church music," ballads, blues, bluegrass, square dancing, and religious music. Describes encountering an unfamiliar style of banjo playing. Centers on Hazard. The trip resulted in issuing of the LP *Mountain Music of Kentucky* (Folkways FA 2317).

252. Combs, Josiah H. "From the Hills to the Sorbonne—and Beyond." *Newsletter of Alice Lloyd College* (July 1975): 11-12.

Notes on the life of the famous song collector.

253. [Combs, Josiah H.] *Kentucky Folklore Record* 6 (1960).

Contains an obituary on Combs, an article by Combs on the music of the southern highlander, the texts to some ballads collected by Combs, and a listing of texts collected by Combs which are in the Western Kentucky University Folklore Archive.

254. French, Katherine Jackson. "A Fortnight in Ballad Country." *Mountain Life and Work* 31, no. 3 (1955): 30-40.

Notes on a collecting trip in eastern Kentucky undertaken by the author in 1909. Several texts.

255. "From Log Cabin School in Kentucky's Feud Country to the Sorbonne . . . and Beyond: Josiah Combs, 1886-1960." *Appalachian Heritage* 2, no. 4 (1974-1975): 55-57.

A short biography of the pioneer collector and scholar of Kentucky folkmusic.

256. Halpert, Violetta Maloney. "Collectors and Students of Folksong, U.S.A." *Southern Folklore Quarterly* 17 (1953): 167-88. Written from Murray. Presents names and addresses of people who have studied folksong in the United States.

257. "Hunting the Lonesome Tune in the Wilds of Kentucky." *Current Opinion* 62 (1917): 100-101.
An article about the fieldwork of Loraine Wyman and Howard Brockway which led to the publication of *Lonesome Tunes: Folksongs of the Kentucky Mountains* [see #241]. Two stanzas illustrate "corruptions and garbled words."

258. "Josephine McGill." *Louisville Library Collections, Biography Series*. Vol. 1, *Artists of Louisville and Kentucky*. Louisville: Louisville Free Public Library, 1939.
Biographical extracts from clippings about McGill's fieldwork in eastern Kentucky and her own musical compositions. Includes a bibliography.

259. Kahn, Ed., "Josiah H. Combs, 1886-1960." *Kentucky Folklore Record* 6 (1960): 101-3.
An obituary with a bibliography of Combs's works.

260. Karpeles, Maud. *Cecil Sharp: His Life and Work*. Chicago: University of Chicago Press, 1967.
A biography of the famous folksong collector, with two chapters on his work in the Appalachians. Includes details of some experiences in Kentucky (at Pineville, Barbourville, Berea, Pine Mountain, and Hindman) and describes singing and dancing at Pine Mountain Settlement School.

261. "List of Collectors and Persons Interested in the Ballad and Folksong Field." *Southern Folklore Quarterly* 1 (1937): 61-73.
A directory, by geographic region, of persons interested in folkmusic and their particular area of interest. Includes some references to Kentucky folkmusic.

262. Lomax, John A. *Adventures of a Ballad Hunter*. New York: Macmillan Co., 1947.
An autobiographical account of song-collecting experiences that mentions traveling in Kentucky. Illustrative stanzas; no melodies.

263. McGee, Nora Dixon. *Kentucky Composers and Compilers of Folk Music: Native and Adopted*. Frankfort, Ky.: State Journal, 1950.
Short biographies of 11 Kentuckians active in the collection and presentation of folkmusic.

264. McGill, Anna Blanche. "On the Trail of Song Ballads." *Kentucky Progress Magazine* 6 (1934): 68-73, 94.
An article about early Kentucky folksong collector Josephine McGill's work with traditional song.

265. ———. "On the Trail of Song Ballets." *Kentucky Folk-Lore and Poetry Magazine* 1, no. 2 (1926): 13-16.
Describes Josephine McGill's historically important collecting experiences in the vicinity of Hindman.

266. McGill, Josephine. "Following Music in a Mountain Land." *Musical Quarterly* 3 (1917): 364-84.
An account of the author's experiences collecting folksongs in the Kentucky mountains, chiefly in Knott County. Sample stanzas, reminiscences about singers, notes on a variety of genres of song.

267. *Notes from the Pine Mountain Settlement School* 2, no. 3 (1924).
Cecil Sharp's legacy at Pine Mountain. Includes a brief mention of hymn singing.

268. Perrow, Eber C. "Background." *Kentucky Folklore Record* 3 (1957): 31-37.
Excerpts from an autobiographical pamphlet by the scholar-collector.

269. "Ree-Collected." *Mountain Life and Work* 2, no. 4 (1927): 29.
Details the reaction of an English couple who collected songs with Cecil Sharp and visited Pine Mountain Settlement School in 1926, where they heard a version of "Little Musgrave."

270. Rothert, Otto. "Josephine McGill—Pioneer in the Kentucky Ballad Field." *Kentucky Folk-Lore and Poetry Magazine* 3, no. 4 (1929): 17-18.
An appreciation of the work of a pioneer song collector (1877-1919). [See #122]

271. Shapiro, Henry D. *Appalachia On Our Mind: The Southern Mountains and Mountaineers in the American Consciousness, 1870-1920*. Chapel Hill: University of North Carolina Press, 1978.
The chapter on the early ballad collectors in Appalachia describes work in Kentucky by Hubert Shearin, E.C. Perrow, Cecil Sharp, Maud Karpeles, and Josephine McGill. Discusses how discovery of the ballad tradition in Appalachia contributed to acceptance of the area as a distinct region and folk culture.

272. Sinclair, Ward. "Getting Kentucky's Talent Together." *Louisville Courier-Journal and Times Magazine,* 24 June 1973, pp. 24-29.

Discusses the roles of Ralph Rinzler, Gerry Davis, and Richard Hulan in locating performers for the 1973 Festival of American Folklife at the Smithsonian Institution, which focused on Kentucky.

273. Smith, Frank H. "Sharp in America." *Mountain Life and Work* 29, no. 4 (1953): 16-17.

More details on Cecil Sharp's experiences in America, and on his influence on the revival of interest in music and dance. No songs or music.

274. Snook, Sidney. "Hill Billy and 'River' Songs at their Source: Notes of an Active Collector in Discovering American Folk Songs." *Etude* 58 (1940): 513.

Describes song collecting in the Kentucky mountains. Focuses on experiences with Aunt Jane Miller and John Carroll, a steamboat pilot.

275. Taylor, Barbara. "Freeman Kitchens and the Freeman Kitchens Collection." *Kentucky Folklore Record* 23 (1977): 12-13.

Describes activities and the vast record collection of a country music enthusiast from Drake, who was instrumental in persuading record companies to reissue material by the Carter family and other early country music performers.

276. Thomas, Jean [Jeannette Bell Thomas]. *The Sun Shines Bright.* New York: Prentice-Hall, 1940.

An autobiography of the "Traipsin' Woman," a court stenographer turned ballad collector and author. Includes illustrative stanzas.

277. ———. *The Traipsin' Woman.* New York: E.P. Dutton and Co., 1933.

An autobiography of the founder of the American Folk Song Festival. Includes a description of the first festival. Fragments of texts, no tunes.

278. Whaley, Charles. "Musicologist Captures the Old Songs from the Hills of Eastern Kentucky." *Louisville Courier-Journal,* 15 July 1960, sec. 1, p. 9.

A description of filmmaker-collector-performer John Cohen's fieldtrip to the Hazard area and the resulting Folkways record *Mountain Music of Kentucky* (Folkways FA 2317). [See also #250-51.]

279. Wilgus, D.K. "Leaders of Kentucky Folklore: Eber C. Perrow, 1880-   ." *Kentucky Folklore Record* 3 (1957): 29-31.
Biographical notes on the former head of the Department of English, University of Louisville, who was a collector of folksongs.

280. ———. "Leaders of Kentucky Folklore: Hubert G. Shearin, 1878-1919." *Kentucky Folklore Record* 2 (1956): 103-4.
Notes on a Kentucky academic who by 1911 had collected more than 400 songs from eastern Kentucky.

281. ———. "Leaders of Kentucky Folklore: Josiah H. Combs." *Kentucky Folklore Record* 3 (1957): 67-69.
A short biography of an important Kentucky scholar-song collector.

282. Williams, Cratis D. "Ballad Collecting in the 1930's." *Appalachian Journal* 7 (1979-80): 33-36.
Describes research and fieldwork the author did for his M.A. thesis, collecting ballads in eastern Kentucky.

283. Wilson, Gordon. "The Problem of Collecting Folk-Lore." *Bulletin of the Kentucky Folk-Lore Society* (July 1932): n.p.
Mentions that the Pennyrile and Jackson Purchase areas are practically untouched by folksong collectors.

Singers, Musicians, and Other Performers

Also see entries: #72, 77, 109, 160, 163, 166, 201, 272, 475, 503, 504, 508, 515, 526-27, 531-32, 543-44, 545-55, 558-60, 563, 573, 579-80, 581, 586-87, 591, 595, 599, 606-7, 611, 650, 654, 658-59, 661, 663-64, 671, 681-87, 690, 703

284. "A Conversation with John McCutcheon." *Mountain Life and Work* 53, no. 10 (1977): 28-29.
McCutcheon, a young folk revivalist musician, came to Kentucky from a school in Minnesota to learn about traditional music at first hand.

285. "Aunt Molly Jackson Memorial Issue." *Kentucky Folklore Record* 7 (1961): 129-76.
A biography of, and obituary for, the well-known folksinger and composer.

286. Ayers, Tom. "'I Feel It Down Through Music': World View in the Titles of Bill Monroe's Recordings." *Journal of Country Music* 6 (1975): 96-108.
Finds a significant correlation between Monroe's world view, as expressed in published interviews and other material, and that reflected in the titles of his recordings. The main themes in both are the family, home and the past, and religion.

287. Baker, Edna Ritchie. "Memories of Musical Moments." *Appalachian Heritage* 5, no. 3 (1977): 59-64.
Autobiographical notes, with illustrative texts (no melodies), by a member of the well-known Ritchie family.

288. "Ballads and Blackberries." *American Magazine* 161 (February 1956): 50-51.
A brief sketch of John Jacob Niles.

289. "Ben Robertson Meets Aunt Molly." *Kentucky Folklore Record* 7 (1961): 133-39.
Part of the memorial issue for Aunt Molly Jackson edited by Archie Green. Includes Green's introduction to a 1931 *New York Herald-Tribune* article by Robertson about Jackson. Derives from Jackson's trip to New York to help the Dreiser

Committee investigate conditions among Harlan County miners. Contains words to one of Jackson's songs.

290. "Bill Monroe: King of Blue Grass Music, Program #1." *Bluegrass Unlimited* 2, no. 5 (November 1967): 4-6.
A transcription of a program produced for Radio McGill, Montreal. Features a general interview with the founder of bluegrass music. [*See also* #291.]

291. "Bill Monroe: King of Blue Grass Music, Program #1, Continued." *Bluegrass Unlimited* 2, no. 6 (December 1967): 3-5.
A continuation of the general interview with Monroe [*see* #290].

292. "Bill Monroe: King of Blue Grass Music, Program #2." *Bluegrass Unlimited* 2, no. 8 (February 1968): 11-12.
A transcription of the second of three radio programs on Monroe. [*See also* #293.]

293. "Bill Monroe: King of Blue Grass Music, Program #2, Continued." *Bluegrass Unlimited* 2, no. 12 (June 1968): 2-5.
A transcription of the second radio program, continued [*see* #292].

294. "Bill Monroe: King of Blue Grass Music, Program #3." *Bluegrass Unlimited* 3, no. 1 (July 1968): 2-4.
A transcription of a radio program featuring an interview with Monroe on the connection between bluegrass and urban audiences.

295. Bolle, Mary Jane. "Happy Medium—J.D. Crowe and the New South." *Bluegrass Unlimited* 8, no. 8 (February 1974): 7-9.
About a Lexington-based bluegrass band that has experimented with progressive approaches.

296. Bowen, Charles G. "Buell Kazee: The Genuine Article." *Sing Out!* 20, no. 2 (1970): 13-17.
A biographical sketch of an eastern Kentucky singer and banjo player who recorded commercially in the 1920s and 1930s. Includes rather detailed information on Kazee's banjo style. Presents one ballad, both text and tune.

297. Brooks, Gwen, and Jim Axelrod. "Roots: Cora Whitaker of Whitaker's Music Store." *Mountain Life and Work* 51, no. 5 (1975): 26-27.
A brief profile of the owner of a record store in Jenkins that features bluegrass, gospel, and old-time country records. No song texts or music.

298. "Bud Meredith: Kentucky Fiddler." *Devil's Box* 10 (1 June 1976): 13-16.

A brief biography of a Grayson County native contest fiddler. Includes tablature for his version of "Anderson's Hornpipe."

299. Burrison, John. "Biography of a Folk Singer: Jean Ritchie." *Folkways Monthly*, January 1963, 4-28.
This biography of the famous singer from Viper includes 10 songs with music.

300. Bussard, Joe, Wilson Reeves, and Leon Kagrise. "Buell Kazee Talking." *Old Time Music* 6 (Autumn 1972): 6-10.
An interview with a singer-banjoist from Magoffin County who began recording in the 1920s.

301. Cantwell, Robert. "Ten Thousand Acres of Bluegrass: Mimesis in Bill Monroe's Music." *Journal of Popular Culture* 13 (1979): 209-20.
Discusses the effects of Bill Monroe's performing style on bluegrass music.

302. "Charlie Monroe." *Bluegrass Unlimited* 10, no. 5 (November 1975): 5.
An obituary for Monroe, 1903-1975.

303. "Clayton McMichen." *Devil's Box* 11 (January 28, 1970): 14.
An obituary for the celebrated hillbilly fiddler who died in Battletown, Meade County.

304. "Clayton McMichen Talking." *Old Time Music* 1 (Summer 1971): 8-10.
An interview with the hillbilly fiddler and famous member of a north Georgia string band, the Skillet Lickers, at his Louisville home in 1959. Focuses on his learning to play the fiddle. [*See also* #305-7.]

305. "Clayton McMichen Talking: 2." *Old Time Music* 2 (Autumn 1971): 13-15.
Covers the early years of McMichen's career—meeting Gid Tanner and playing on the radio.

306. "Clayton McMichen Talking: 3." *Old Time Music* 3 (Winter 1971-72): 14-15, 19.
Discusses McMichen's playing with the Skillet Lickers.

307. "Clayton McMichen Talking: 4." *Old Time Music* 4 (Spring 1971): 19-20, 30.
Focuses primarily on the fiddler's repertoire.

308. Cobb, Alice. "The Ballad Singer." *Notes from Pine Mountain Settlement School* 7, no. 2 (1935): n.p.
Notes on traditional singer Lige Jackson, from Pine Mountain, include three texts with melodies. [*See also* #50.]

309. Coltman, Robert. " 'Sweethearts of the Hills': Women in Early Country Music." *JEMF Quarterly* 14 (1978): 161-80.
Surveys the contributions of women performers in country music in the 1920s and 1930s, including the Coon Creek Girls, the Kentucky Girls, and other Kentucky performers.

310. Connor, Bob. "Quick with the Bow." *Mountain Life and Work* 37, no. 4 (1961): 7-12.
A look at the many talents of Ralph Marcum, a schoolteacher at Sand Gap. Marcum, a fiddler, was a regular cast member on the Renfro Valley weekly country music show. No tunes or texts.

311. Coppage, Noel. "John Jacob Niles: How to Make Your Mark on the Folk Music Process with 'the Electric Effect of the Male Alto C Sharp.' " *Stereo Review* 34, no. 1 (1975): 56-61.
A profile of John Jacob Niles at age eighty-two; his reflections on his career and thoughts on dulcimers, death, and the "folk process."

312. Daniel, Wayne. "From Barn Dance to Recording Company Executive: The Story of Cotton Carrier." *JEMF Quarterly* 15 (1979): 230-36.
The life and career of a hillbilly performer from the Mammoth Cave area, covering the 1930s through the present.

313. Davis, Chandler. "Bluegrass Family—Family Bluegrass." *Bluegrass Unlimited* 7, no. 4 (October 1972): 5-8.
A biographical account of the McLain Family bluegrass band with information on family members and the band's career.

314. Davis, Stephen F. "Jilson Setters: The Man of Many Names." *Devil's Box* 12 (March 1, 1978): 42-45.
Examines the way in which Jean Thomas, the author and festival producer from Ashland, created the Jilson Setters persona for fiddler J.W. ("Blind Bill") Day. Includes a discography of 1928 Victor recordings and subsequent field recordings for the Archive of Folk Song, the Library of Congress.

315. ———. "Uncle Bert Layne." *Devil's Box* 26 (September 1, 1974): 19-24.
A biography of an Arkansas native who fiddled with the Skillet Lickers from north Georgia, and retired to Covington, ca. 1940.

316. Dellar, Fred. *The Illustrated Encyclopedia of Country Music.* New York: Harmony Books, 1977.
Capsule descriptions of the careers of country music perform-

ers from the 1920s to the 1970s. Discographies included for many performers.

317. "Dulcimer Maker." *Scenic South,* August 1955, 16-20.
A picture story on Jethro Amburgey, a Hindman craftsman.

318. Earle, Gene. "The Cliff Carlisle Story." *Folk Style* 7 [n.d.]: 3-21.
A biography of a Spencer County hillbilly performer, based on an interview at his suburban Lexington home. Features Carlisle's performing and recording careers, his major song folios, and brief notes on his life in retirement. A lengthy discography for Cliff and his younger brother Bill is appended. [*See also* #655.]

319. Edens, George C. "Southern Melody Boys." *Old Time Music* 13 (Summer 1974): 13-15.
A history of this hillbilly duet. Includes a biography of banjo player Joseph Odus Maggard, a Hazard native. With discography.

320. "England Sings for a Kentucky Girl." *Louisville Courier-Journal,* 20 September 1953, section 4.
Singer Jean Ritchie performs and does research into her musical traditions in Ireland and England.

321. "Folk Music Recital Set at Western Tomorrow." *Park City Daily News* [Bowling Green, Ky.], 17 October 1961, p. 5.
A notice of an upcoming concert at Western Kentucky State College (now University) by Edna Ritchie of Viper. [*See also* #324, 325.]

322. "Folk Singer." *Life,* 6 September 1940, 57-60.
A biographical piece on John Jacob Niles, whose songs are considered especially meaningful during World War II.

323. "Folk Singer 'Aunt Polly' Triplett, of 'Traipsin' Woman' Troupe, Dies." *Louisville Courier-Journal,* 13 December 1957, n.p.
An obituary for an eastern Kentucky singer and dulcimer player who was part of Jean Thomas's troupe of performers.

324. "Folksinger Sings for Chapel Assembly." [Western Kentucky State College] *College Heights Herald,* 25 October 1961, p. 3.
An account of a campus concert by Edna Ritchie. [*See also* #321, 325.]

325. "Folksinger to Perform on Campus October 18." [Western Kentucky State College] *College Heights Herald,* 11 October 1961, p. 3.

A notice of an upcoming concert by Edna Ritchie of Viper. With photo. [*See also* #321, 324.]

326. Foster, Alice, ed. "Growing Up in Rosine, Kentucky: An Interview with Bill Monroe." *Sing Out!* 19, no. 2 (1969): 6-11.

An interview with the "Father of Bluegrass" music recorded in Nashville in 1969. Focuses on Monroe's youth. Includes text to "Uncle Pen," Monroe's song about his musically influential uncle.

327. ————. "Kenny Baker." *Bluegrass Unlimited* 3, no. 6 (December 1968): 8-11.

A biography of a Jenkins native, a fiddler with Bill Monroe. Taken from a 1968 interview.

328. ————. "Sam Bush." *Bluegrass Unlimited* 4, no. 5 (November 1969): 11-12.

About a young instrumentalist (fiddle and mandolin) from south-central Kentucky, later leader of New Grass Revival.

329. Gaillard, Frye. *Watermelon Wine: The Spirit of Country Music.* New York: St. Martin's Press, 1978.

Examines country music's relationship with traditional music, creativity, and commercialism. Includes information on Kentucky performers Asa Martin, Bradley Kincaid, Buell Kazee, Merle Travis, and Tom T. Hall.

330. Garland, Jim. "It Seems to Me . . . ." *Sing Out!* 16, no. 5 (1966): 10-15.

A semiautobiographical article with illustrative song stanzas and two full song texts.

331. Godbey, Marty. "Bluegrass, Bluegrass . . . : A Television Series." *Bluegrass Unlimited* 12, no. 5 (November 1977): 9-11.

Kentucky Educational Television produces a series featuring noted bluegrass bands.

332. ————. "Riverfront Bluegrass." *Bluegrass Unlimited* 10, no. 9 (March 1976): 12-14.

About the popular band Bluegrass Alliance, based at a club in Louisville.

333. Green, Archie. "A Discography/Biography Journey: The Martin-Roberts-Martin 'Aggregation.' " *Western Folklore* 30 (1971): 194-201.

Describes how preparation of a hillbilly discography led to discovery of, and a personal glimpse into the lives of, seven old-time musicians in Kentucky.

334. ————. "A Folklorist's Creed and Folksinger's Gift." *Appalachian Journal* 7 (1979-1980): 37-45.

Reflections on the role of Kentucky folksinger Sarah Ogan Gunning in Appalachian political and cultural events, including the 1930s mining struggles in eastern Kentucky.

335. ———. "Bradley Kincaid's Folios." *JEMF Quarterly* 13 (1977): 21-28.
Kincaid, a well-known early radio performer, began issuing songbooks in 1919, eventaully publishing about 14 folios by 1948. Illustrated.

336. ———. "Mary Magdalene Stewart Jackson Stamos: 1880-1960." *Kentucky Folklore Record* 7 (1961): 129-30.
Biographical notes on Aunt Molly Jackson, an eastern Kentucky singer active in social struggles.

337. Greene, Robert Bruce. "Henry L. Bandy: The Old-Time Fiddler." *Kentucky Folklore Record* 18 (1972): 99-102.
A biography of an archaic fiddler from Allen County who made a number of hillbilly records.

338. Greenway, John. "Aunt Molly Jackson as an Informant." *Kentucky Folklore Record* 7 (1961):141-46.
Describes the celebrated traditional singer and songwriter as an informant for folklorists.

339. Griffen, Gerald. "Quite a Looker-on-the-Dark-Side is Knott's Balladeer-Legislator." *Louisville Courier-Journal*, 26 January 1956, sec. 1, p. 7.
"Banjo Bill" Cornett from Hindman is elected to the state legislature on the strength of his banjo playing and singing.

340. Griffis, Ken. "The Roy Lanham Story." *JEMF Quarterly* 10 (1974): 165-68.
A biography and discography of a country music entertainer who is a Corbin native.

341. Guthrie, Charles S. " 'Whitey' Stearns: Troubador of the Cumberland Valley." *Kentucky Folklore Record* 18 (1972): 52-55.
This biography of a Kentucky musician includes 94 titles in his repertoire.

342. Guthrie, Woody. *American Folksong*. New York: Oak Publications, 1961.
A songbook that includes reminiscences about Aunt Molly Jackson, Jim Garland, and Sarah Ogan (Gunning)—all singers from eastern Kentucky.

343. Harlow, Alvin F. *Weep No More My Lady*. New York: Whittlesey House, 1942.
The chapter entitled "Mountain Songstress" (pp. 242-55) portrays Aunt Molly Jackson. Includes texts, words only, for two

Jackson compositions—an untitled local ballad, her first composition, and "Miners' Wives Ragged Hungry Blues."

344. Henderson, Connie. "They Called Him 'Singing' Billy." *Mountain Life and Work* 38 (1962): 49-52.

The life and work of William Walker, author of a number of shape-note hymnals, including *Southern Harmony* (1825). Mentions the annual singing at Benton.

345. High, Ellesa Clay. "The Coon Creek Girl from Red River Gorge: An Interview with Lily May Pennington." *Adena* 2, no. 1 (1977): 44-74.

Lily May talks about her life and career with the Coon Creek Girls and her feelings about bluegrass, country, and folkmusic.

346. Howard, John Tasker. *Stephen Foster: America's Troubador.* New York: Thomas Y. Crowell Co., 1934.

A biography of the songwriter with a list of Foster's published works.

347. Hustlin' Dan. "The Falls City Ramblers." *Bluegrass Unlimited* 9, no. 4 (October 1974): 21-22.

Notes on a Louisville bluegrass band.

348. "Jean Ritchie." *Hillbilly-Folk Record Journal* 2 (1955): 5-6.

A brief biographical article.

349. "Jim Garland: In Memory and Honor." *Mountain Life and Work* 54, no. 9 (1978): 36.

An obituary of a singer and songwriter who helped organize Kentucky miners in the 1930s.

350. Jones, Loyal, "Buell Kazee." *JEMF Quarterly* 14 (1978): 57-67.

An overview of Kazee's career as folksinger and banjo player, and remarks on his singing and playing style. Based on an interview done in the early 1970s.

351. ———. "Jean Ritchie, Twenty-Five Years After." *Appalachian Journal* 8 (1980-81): 224-29.

A review essay of Ritchie's *High Hills and Mountains* album and her book *Singing Family of the Cumberlands.* Discusses the influence of Ritchie's music in rallying support for the preservation of Appalachian culture. Includes a bibliography/discography.

352. ———. *Radio's "Kentucky Mountain Boy" Bradley Kincaid.* Berea, Ky.: Berea College Appalachian Center, 1980.

A portrait of Kincaid's life and career, followed by words and music to 50 songs from his repertoire. Appendices include an annotated checklist of Kincaid's song repertoire, a list of songbooks published by Kincaid, and a discography of Kincaid's recordings.

353. ———. "Who Is Bradley Kincaid?" *JEMF Quarterly* 12 (1976): 122-37.
The life and career of this popular Kentucky singer and radio personality.

354. Kaplan, Kathy. "Charlie Monroe (1903-1975)." *Sing Out!* 24, no. 4 (1975): 25-26.
An obituary for this Rosine musician, a member of the Monroe Brothers.

355. "Kentucky Blues: Part One." *Living Blues,* no. 51 (Summer 1981): 25-36.
Short articles by Jim O'Neal, Burnham Ware, and Burt Feintuch on several older black musicians from rural Kentucky and the jug bands of Louisville.

356. "Kentucky's Ancient Minstrel Wanders Afar from His Folks." *Literary Digest,* 24 December 1932, pp. 26-27.
A biographical sketch of 74-year-old Kentucky fiddler Jilson Setters as he is about to embark on a trip to England to perform at the National Festival of Folk Song in London.

357. Kirby, Rich. "George Tucker: . . . 'Learning Our Children More Mountain Music.' " *Mountain Life and Work* 48, no. 11 (1972): 8-10.
An interview with a Letcher County musician.

358. Kuykendall, Pete. "James Monroe." *Bluegrass Unlimited* 8, no. 1 (July 1973): 9-12.
The career of Bill Monroe's son, a bluegrass vocalist and guitarist who played with his father's band until he formed his own.

359. ———. "The Osborne Brothers: From Rocky Top to Muddy Bottom." *Bluegrass Unlimited* 12, no. 6 (December 1977): 10-16.
Focuses on the later career of these Hyden natives, bluegrass innovators.

360. Ladd, Bill. "The Home Town Smokes Travis Out." *Louisville Courier-Journal Magazine,* 16 November 1947, pp. 6-8.
Merle Travis helps raise funds for a playground in Drakesboro, his home town, by doing local concerts.

361. Lauck, Rex. "Merle Travis Day!" *United Mine Workers Journal* 67 (15 July 1956): 10-11.
A celebration in Ebenezer for the unveiling of a monument to Travis, attended by 12,000 people.

362. Lawless, Ray M. *Folksingers and Folksongs in America.* New York: Duell, Sloan and Pearce, 1960.
Includes biographies of a number of prominent Kentucky singers, such as Jean Ritchie, Bradley Kincaid, and Buell Kazee.

363. Lawrence, Keith. "Arnold Shultz: The Greatest? Guitar Picker's Life Ended before Promise Realized." *JEMF Quarterly* 17 (1981): 3-8.
Reprint of an Owensboro *Messenger-Inquirer* article on a black Ohio County guitarist who influenced Bill Monroe, Mose Rager, and others with his thumb-pick style.

364. Lawson, Ernie. *52 Years of Uncle Bozo of the Original Carver Family.* Burkesville, Ky.: n.p., 1965.
Copy not available for verification of citation or annotation. Uncle Bozo (Noble Carver) was a hillbilly performer who recorded with family members for Paramount, ca. 1927.

365. Ledford, Lily May. *Coon Creek Girl.* Berea, Ky.: Berea College Appalachian Center, 1980.
A short autobiography of the lead performer and banjo player of the Coon Creek Girls, an early all-woman country band.

366. Lightfoot, William. "Mose Rager of Muhlenberg County: 'Hey, c'mon bud, play me a good rag.' " *Adena* 4 (1979): 3-41.
An interview with the Drakesboro guitarist, an exemplar of western Kentucky "choke-style" guitar picking.

367. Lomax, Alan. "Aunt Molly Jackson: An Appreciation." *Kentucky Folklore Record* 7 (1961): 131-32.
An obituary.

368. Ludden, Keith J. " 'If It's on the Radio, Why Bother': A Study of Two Southeast Barren County, Kentucky Ballad Singers." *Kentucky Folklore Record* 24 (1978): 54-60.
Focuses on Clorine Lawson and Gladys Pace, two singers representative of south-central Kentucky traditional balladry. Discusses the importance of music in their lives.

369. McCleary, Anna L. "My Old Kentucky Home: An Eighty-Five Year Old Folk Song and Something of Its History." *Etude* 57 (1939): 299.
Biographical data on Stephen C. Foster, including accounts of his wedding, his death, and the circumstances of his writing "My Old Kentucky Home."

370. McCord, Merrill. "Musical Comeback." *Louisville Courier-Journal Magazine*, 11 December 1960, pp. 7-8.

On the popularity of bluegrass music and the role of Ohio County native Bill Monroe.

371. Malone, Bill C., and Judith McCulloh, eds. *Stars of Country Music.* Urbana: University of Illinois Press, 1975.
Includes a chapter on Bradley Kincaid, written by D.K. Wilgus, and references to other Kentucky performers.

372. Marshall, John. "Earlie Botts." *Kentucky Folklore Record* 24 (1978): 81-88.
A profile of a traditional singer and musician from Monroe County, Kentucky. Botts plays banjo left-handed and claims to be one of only a few remaining practitioners of the "standing hand" style of banjo playing.

373. Martin, Mac. "Bill Monroe and the Fiddle." *Bluegrass Unlimited* 3, no. 8 (February 1969): 6-8.
Notes on fiddlers who have played with Monroe's band.

374. Maynard, Donna. "New Grass: The Bloomin' Grass." *Bluegrass Unlimited* 12, no. 1 (July 1977): 39-41.
Discusses a young bluegrass band formed in 1974 in Morehead.

375. Nash, Allanna. "Sam Bush, New Grass Revival and Leon Russell." *Bluegrass Unlimited* 8, no. 4 (October 1973): 22-23.
About a native bluegrass mandolinist-fiddler-singer, his progressive band, and their tour with a rock star.

376. Nelson, Donald Lee. "John V. Walker: Corbin's Finest." *JEMF Quarterly* 8 (1972): 133-39.
A biography and discography of a hillbilly fiddler and banjo player from Corbin.

377. ———. "The Life of Alfred G. Karnes." *JEMF Quarterly* 8 (1972): 31-36.
A biography of the 1920s hillbilly singer who lived most of his life in Kentucky.

378. ———. "McVay and Johnson." *JEMF Quarterly* 10 (1974): 92-95.
The lives and careers of hillbilly duet Ancil McVay, from Corbin, and Roland Johnson, from Clay County, who first recorded as accompanists for Ernest Phipps in 1927. With photographs and discography.

379. "Passing of Jilson Setters, The." *Arcadian Life* 54 (September 1942): 15, 22.
An obituary for Jilson Setters (Blind Bill Day), a Rowan County native, 1861-1942. Includes texts, words only, for "Show

Pity, Lord, Oh Lord Forgive," reportedly his favorite hymn, and a funerary poem by Blanche Preston Jones.

380. Price, Steven D. *Old as the Hills: The Story of Bluegrass Music.* New York: Viking, 1975.
A popuar history of bluegrass music. Includes a chapter devoted to Bill Monroe, the music's founder, from Rosine.

381. Provo, Clifford. "Bill Monroe Honored by Kentucky." *Bluegrass Unlimited* 4, no. 6 (December 1969): 2.
Governor Nunn proclaims Bill Monroe Day in Kentucky.

382. Reeves, Florence. "A Kentucky Ballad Singer." *Mountain Life and Work* 12, no. 4 (1937): 18-19.
A biographical sketch of Aunt Phronnie, a singer from Lone Wolf Branch who was a source for Cecil Sharp.

383. Riddle, Margaret. "A Skillet-Licker's Memoirs: Bert Layne." *Old Time Music* 14 (Autumn 1974): 5-9.
An interview with a former member of a north Georgia string band, the Skillet Lickers, who retired to Covington. [*See also* #384.]

384. ———. "A Skillet-Licker's Memoirs, Part 2: Bert Layne." *Old Time Music* 15 (Winter 1974-75): 22-24.
A continuation of the interview [*see* #383.]

385. Ridenour, George L. *Early Times in Meade County, Kentucky.* Louisville: Western Recorder, 1929.
A brief description of the singing and preaching of a Brother Hicks from Mount Pleasant Church (p. 107). When singing or preaching Hicks could reportedly be heard all the way across the Ohio River.

386. Rinzler, Ralph. "Bill Monroe—Thirty Years." *Bluegrass Unlimited* 4, no. 4 (October 1969): 2-4.
An appreciation on the occasion of Monroe's thirtieth anniversary on the Grand Old Opry.

387. Ritchie, Edna [Edna Ritchie Baker]. "The Singing Ritchies." *Mountain Life and Work* 29, no. 3 (1953): 6-10.
Memories of childhood in a singing family. Contains illustrative fragments of song texts.

388. Ritchie, Jean. "Jean Ritchie's Junaluska Keynote: Now Is the Cool of the Day." *Mountain Life and Work* 46, no. 5 (1970): 3-8.
A keynote address that focuses on the relationship between the singer's work, songs, and life.

389. ———. "Living Is Collecting: Growing Up in a Southern Appalachian 'Folk' Family." In *An Appalachian Symposium:*

Essays Written in Honor of Cratis D. Williams, ed. J.W. Williamson. Boone, N.C.: Appalachian State University Press, 1977.

Recalls the rich folkmusic tradition of the Ritchie clan, especially the repertoires of Balis and Jason Ritchie. Presents texts of three previously unpublished songs from Jason Ritchie's repertoire.

390. ———. *Singing Family of the Cumberlands.* New York: Oxford University Press, 1955.

An autobiography by this singing family's most famous member. Presents a variety of songs, with music, framed by the context of family history.

391. ———. "Yonder Comes My Beau." *Ladies Home Journal* 72 (April 1955): 54, 127-29.

An excerpt from *Singing Family of the Cumberlands* centering on courtship. [*See* #390.]

392. Roberts, Leonard. *Up Cutshin and Down Greasy: Folkways of a Kentucky Mountain Family.* Lexington: University of Kentucky Press, 1959.

A study of "the simple history and folkways of this mountain family [the Couch family], their daily life in work and play, in joy and sorrow." Includes texts and music for a number of ballads and lyric folksongs, with annotations. From fieldwork done in 1952. [*See also* #480.]

393. Rooney, James. *Bossmen: Bill Monroe and Muddy Waters.* New York: Dial Press, 1971.

Bill Monroe's career in bluegrass, much of it told in his own words. He talks about musical influences on him as he was growing up in Kentucky. Includes texts of some of his songs.

394. Rosenberg, Neil. "The Osborne Brothers, Part One—Family and Apprenticeship." *Bluegrass Unlimited* 6, no. 3 (September 1971): 5-10.

Focuses on the family life and early career of the brothers from Hyden, leading bluegrass musicians. [*See also* #395.]

395. ———. "The Osborne Brothers, Part Two—Getting It Off." *Bluegrass Unlimited* 6, no. 8 (February 1972): 5-8.

Covers the period ca. 1956-1962. [*See* #394.]

396. Russell, Tony. "Buell Kazee, 1900-1976." *Old Time Music* 21 (Summer 1976): 17-18.

An obituary for the renowned singer, hillbilly recording artist, banjo player, and minister.

397. ———. "Dick Burnett." *Old Time Music* 23 (Winter 1976-77): 4.
An obituary for the Monticello fiddler.

398. Schulman, Steven A. "Howess Dewey Winfrey: The Rejected Songmaker." *Journal of American Folklore* 87 (1974): 72-84.
A study of a satirical songmaker from Cumberland County and his songs. Based on fieldwork with the singer in 1972. Gives eight complete or partial texts; no melodies.

399. ———. "Reminiscence of Logging along the Cumberland." *Kentucky Folklore Record* 18 (1972): 96-98.
Memories of logging in Cumberland County in the 1920s from an elderly informant. Includes one text with a note that it is sung to the tune of "Casey Jones."

400. Silber, Irwin, and David Gahr. "Top Performers Highlight 1st Newport Folk Fest." *Sing Out!* 9, no. 2 (1959): 21-24.
Mentions Kentuckians Jean Ritchie and John Jacob Niles among other performers.

401. Sims, Vincent. "The Red Allen Story." *Bluegrass Unlimited* 2, no. 2 (August 1967): 2-3.
The life of a bluegrass musician and native of Bulan, near Hazard, focusing on his professional career.

402. Smith, Jo Anne Peden. "William Goebel Twyman: Hart County's Old-Time Fiddler." *Kentucky Folklore Record* 21 (1975): 82-84.
Discusses highlights of Twyman's long career as a country musician—early musical influences, playing for square dances, performing on the radio, recording an album and forming a band with other family members.

403. "Sonny Tells It Like It Is." *Bluegrass Unlimited* 3, no. 12 (June 1969): 7-15.
An interview with Hyden native and bluegrass banjoist Sonny Osborne on the state of bluegrass music.

404. Sweeney, Margaret. "Mrs. Ernest Shope: A Memorable Informant." *Kentucky Folklore Record* 11 (1965): 17-24.
Three ballads collected from a Taylor County native. No melodies.

405. Taylor, David L. "They Like to Sing the Old Songs: The A.L. Phipps Family and Its Music." M.A. thesis, Western Kentucky University, 1978.
An ethnographic study of the secular music, sacred songs, and performance career of the Phipps family of Barbourville. In-

cludes texts to several songs from the family's repertoire and a discography.

406. ———. "They Like to Sing the Old Songs: An Introduction to the A.L. Phipps Family and their Music." *JEMF Quarterly* 13 (1977): 29-37.
An overview of this performing family from Barbourville who have been inspired by the Carter Family, early country music stars.

407. Taylor, Jay. "Bradley Kincaid: Still the 'Kentucky Mountain Boy' at 81." *Kentucky Folklore Record* 24 (1978): 10-14.
A brief overview of Kincaid's career on radio and records as well as his contribution to American country music.

408. Thierman, Sue McClelland. "Young Man with a Guitar: Logan English of Bourbon County Has Recorded Three Albums of Kentucky Folk Songs, and His Future Looks Bright." *Louisville Courier-Journal Magazine*, 2 November 1958, p. 10.
This folk revivalist singer's musical accomplishments.

409. Thomas, Jean [Jeannette Bell Thomas]. "A Mountain Minstrel Goes to London Town." *Arcadian Life* 1 (January 1935): 1, 8-9.
The author recounts her experiences with "Jilson Setters, The Singin' Fiddler of Lost Hope Hollow" (Blind Bill Day). Focus is on Setters's performances in London for the English Folk Dance and Song Society.

410. ———. *The Singin' Fiddler of Lost Hope Hollow.* New York: E.P. Dutton, 1938.
A romanticized biography of mountain fiddler Jilson Setters (Blind Bill Day). Includes texts; no music.

411. Thompson, Eloise, and [William] Lynwood Montell. "Uncle Henry and the Kentucky Mountaineers." *Kentucky Folklore Record* 15 (1969): 29-34.
A biography of Uncle Henry Warren, a Green County Native, that emphasizes his hillbilly music career.

412. Tottle, Jack. "Ricky Skaggs: Clinch Mountain to Boone Creek." *Bluegrass Unlimited* 11, no. 7 (January 1977): 8-16.
The career of a young bluegrass musician and native of Cordell. Skaggs played with Ralph Stanley and then formed his own band.

413. Travis, James. "John Jacob Niles: A Voice from Kentucky." *Southern Living* 4, no. 6 (1969): 62-66.
Discusses Niles's contributions as a folk musician, ballad re-

searcher, poet, dulcimer maker, painter, and composer. Based on an interview with Niles.

414. Travis, Merle. "The Saga of 'Sixteen Tons': I Owe My Soul to the Company Store." *United Mine Workers Journal* 66 (1 December 1955): 5-6.
An autobiographical statement, with emphasis on music and mining, by the author of "Sixteen Tons."

415. Tribe, Ivan M. "Charlie Monroe." *Bluegrass Unlimited* 10, no. 4 (October 1975): 12-19.
The life and career of this Rosine native and hillbilly era recording artist, later leader of the Kentucky Pardners.

416. ———. "Fiddling Doc Roberts." *Devil's Box* 10 (1 March 1976): 43-45.
A brief biography of a celebrated eastern Kentucky fiddler.

417. ———. "Goins Brothers: Melvin and Ray—Maintaining the Lonesome Pine Fiddler Tradition." *Bluegrass Unlimited* 8, no. 11 (1974): 11-18.
Ray and Melvin Goins are eastern Kentucky natives and bluegrass musicians.

418. ———. "Hylo Brown: The Bluegrass Balladeer." *Bluegrass Unlimited* 9, no. 2 (August 1974): 10-13.
About a Johnson County native who went on to a country music career.

419. ———. "Jimmie Skinner: Country Singer, Bluegrass Composer, Record Retailer." *Bluegrass Unlimited* 11, no. 9 (March 1977): 34-37.
About a Madison County native's musical career.

420. ———, and John W. Morris. "Molly O'Day and Lynn Davis: A Strong Influence on Bluegrass Music." *Bluegrass Unlimited* 9, no. 3 (September 1974): 10-15.
An examination of the careers of two natives of eastern Kentucky who became influential country musicians.

421. Wagoner, James. "Lawrence Lane and the Kentucky Grass." *Bluegrass Unlimited* 10, no. 1 (July 1975): 22-25.
About the Somerset area leader of a bluegrass band, now a resident of Marion, Ohio.

422. Ward, Edward, and Robert Coltman. "Music in Harlan County, Kentucky: Reminiscences of a Long-Time Resident." *JEMF Quarterly* 15 (1979): 20-26.
A lifelong resident of Harlan County, Ed Ward, remembers life and music in Straight Creek during the 1910s and 1920s. He discusses local old-time musicians, entertainment in pre-radio

days, including traveling minstrels and running sets, and the arrival of the phonograph.

423. "When the Angels Carry Me Home: A Tribute to Charlie Monroe." *Devil's Box* 9 (1 December 1975): 43-44.

An obituary for the Rosine native and early country musician, one of the Monroe Brothers.

424. "Which Side Are You On? An Interview with Florence Reece." *Mountain Life and Work* 48, no. 3 (1972): 22-24.

Reprint of a *Sing Out!* interview in which Reece explains the events that led her to write "Which Side Are You On?" Includes text and tune of the song, plus two others that Reece wrote.

425. Wilson, Gail. "Country Music: That Kentucky Sound!" *Kentucky Heritage* 13, no. 3 (1973): 8-9.

A short history of country music in Kentucky, focusing on some of the performers who have gained fame in the past 50 years, from Bradley Kincaid and Buell Kazee to the Osborne Brothers and Loretta Lynn.

426. Wilson, Gordon. *Fidelity Folks*. Cynthiana, Ky.: Hobson Book Press, 1946.

A series of short articles about the people of Fidelity, Kentucky, and their lives. Includes a number of ballads, a description of "Aunt Jane," a ballad singer, and notes on domestic singing sessions.

427. Wilson, Mark, and Guthrie Meade. "Buddy Thomas, Kentucky Fiddler." *Old Time Music* 21 (Summer 1976): 7-11.

An interview with a fiddler from Emerson, in northeastern Kentucky, who had a striking repertoire of old-time tunes. Also published as liner notes to Thomas's Rounder l.p. (0032), *Kitty Puss: Old-Time Fiddle Music from Kentucky*.

428. Wolfe, Charles K. "Bluegrass Touches: An Interview with Bill Monroe." *Old Time Music* 16 (Spring 1975): 6-12.

The "Father of Bluegrass Music" discusses his early musical influences, his early career, recordings made with his brother, fiddlers, the influence of black musicians on his music, and the Grand Ole Opry.

429. ———. "Ernie Hodges: From Coal Creek to Bach." *Devil's Box* 9 (1 June 1975): 22-41.

An interview with a fiddler whose career involved him with a number of musical genres. Hodges was a longtime Kentucky resident.

430. ———. "McMichen in Kentucky: The Sunset Years." *Devil's Box* 11 (1 June 1977): 10-18.
An examination of Clayton McMichen's years in Kentucky, ca. 1960-1970, a period described as his comeback years, characterized by the folk revival interest in his fiddling.

431. ———. "Man of Constant Sorrow: Richard Burnett's Story." *Old Time Music* 9 (Summer 1973): 6-9.
An interview with the blind fiddler from Monticello who recorded classic duets with banjoist Leonard Rutherford, 1926-1930. [See also #432.]

432. ———. "Man of Constant Sorrow: Richard Burnett's Story." *Old Time Music* 10 (Autumn 1973): 5-9.
This continuation of an interview [see #431] features discussions of traveling, recording, learning songs, other musicians, and Burnett's songbook.

433. ———. "Tracking the Lost String Bands." *Southern Exposure* 5, no. 2-3 (1977): 11-20.
Looks at some of the performers who were in the southern string bands during the 1920s and 1930s, including Kentuckians Dick Burnett and Leonard Rutherford.

Text - Centered Studies

Also see entries: #64, 286, 510

434. Ashby, Rickie Zayne. "The Possum Hunters in the Oral Tradition." *Kentucky Folklore Record* 21 (1975): 56-61.
Demonstrates the validity of folksongs as historical sources. Uses two texts from Ohio County as aids in researching the history of the Possum Hunters, a terrorist vigilante group in western Kentucky in the years preceding World War I.

435. Averill, Patricia Anne. "Can the Circle Be Unbroken: A Study of the Modernization of Rural Born Southern Whites since World War I Using Country Music." Ph.D. dissertation, University of Pennsylvania, 1975.
Examines 2,000 country song lyrics from 1928-1938, 1953, and 1968 for evidence of changes in the world view of rural southern-born whites.

436. Boswell, George W. "The Five Phase [*sic*] Folk Tune." *Kentucky Folklore Record* 15 (1969): 3-11.
Examines five-phrase melodies, in which a fifth line is added to a melody which is basically four lines. Focuses on ballads from the areas covered by Sharp, as well as Boswell's own collected materials from Tennessee. Includes graphs of tunes and phrasal characteristics.

437. Bradley, William Aspenwell. "Song-Ballets and Devil's Ditties." *Harpers Monthly Magazine* 130 (May 1915): 901-14.
Discusses the rich tradition of old ballads existing in eastern Kentucky and predicts their demise as literacy increases. Includes anecdotes of informal musical gatherings and a description of the dulcimer.

438. Campbell, John C. *The Southern Highlander and His Homeland.* New York: Russell Sage Foundation, 1921.
A classic study of the southern Appalachians. Includes texts from Sharp's fieldwork and hymns from Billings's *The Sweet Songster.* Some descriptive material dealing with hymn-singing, fiddling, dulcimers, and dancing may be from Kentucky.

439. Campbell, Marie. "Feuding Ballads from the Kentucky Mountains." *Southern Folklore Quarterly* 3 (1969): 165-72.

Presents a short overview of attitudes toward feuding in the mountains along with a number of common feuding songs, from one informant from Carcassone. Texts only; no melodies.

440. ————. "The Folklife of a Kentucky Mountain Community." M.A. thesis, Peabody College, 1937.
Contains a large number and variety of song texts from the vicinity of Gander, Letcher County. The author attempts to describe folklore in the context of everyday life in the community.

441. ————. "Liquor Ballads from the Kentucky Mountains." *Southern Folklore Quarterly* 2 (1938): 157-64.
Texts of drinking songs collected in Gander, Bull Creek, and Elk Creek. Drinking songs were generally sung covertly rather than at community gatherings or in the presence of strangers. No melodies.

442. Cohen, Anne B. *Poor Pearl, Poor Girl!* Austin: University of Texas Press, 1978.
Focuses on the 1896 murder of Pearl Bryan, the basis for a number of ballads. Compares the ballads with newspaper accounts of the crime and concludes that both were based on, or influenced by, formulaic notions having to do with murdered girls and criminals brought to justice. Materials come primarily from Kentucky, Indiana, and Ohio. First written as an M.A. thesis at UCLA.

443. Cohen, Norm. *Long Steel Rail: The Railroad in American Folksong.* Urbana: University of Illinois Press, 1980.
An anthology of railroad songs with text and tune. Material is drawn mainly from commercial recordings, especially hillbilly and blues records from 1920 to 1950. Extensive notes identify other versions, including unpublished texts and field recordings in archives. Western Kentucky Folklore Archive at UCLA and Berea College Library contributed material.

444. Combs, Josiah H. *Folk Songs du Midi des Etats-Unis.* Paris: Les Presses Universitaires de France, 1925.
A doctoral dissertation in French, with song texts in English, which formed the basis of the later edition edited by D.K. Wilgus [see #445]. From West Virginia and from Knott, Perry, and Breathitt counties, Kentucky.

445. ————. *Folk-Songs of the Southern United States.* Ed. D.K. Wilgus. Publications of the American Folklore Society, Bibliographical and Special Series, vol. 19. Austin: University of Texas Press, 1968.

A translation of Combs's 1925 dissertation done at the University of Paris [see #444]. Part I discusses topography, ancestry, song origins and authorship, field research, the classification of songs, native American songs, the highlander's music, songs of British origin, and "the passing of the folk-song." Part II presents 60 texts, all without music. Gives Laws and Child numbers where appropriate, brief headnotes, and information on informants. Includes discussions of the fiddle and the mountain dulcimer. Deals with the southern highland region, including eastern Kentucky.

446. ———. "The Highlander's Music." *Kentucky Folklore Record* 6 (1960): 108-22.
Outlines and discusses the types of music in the southern highlands. Focuses on three instruments, the fiddle, banjo, and dulcimer. Also discusses the use of gapped scales by singers. D.K. Wilgus provides an introductory note.

447. Coppage, Noel. "Fights, Fiddles, and Foxhunts." *Kentucky Folklore Record* 7 (1961): 1-14.
Presents narratives concerning fighting, fiddling, and foxhunting from Ohio and Grayson counties. Discusses the role of the local fiddler, focusing on dances, ice cream suppers, and other social occasions. Provides one stanza from each of five fiddle tunes.

448. Foss, George, and Roger D. Abrahams. "Fair Nottalin Town." *Kentucky Folklore Record* 14 (1968): 88-91.
A short study of a nonsense song collected in Knott County by Foss. With music and comparative notes.

449. Gaines, Ray. "The Legend of Long John Dean." *Park City Daily News* [Bowling Green, Ky.], 16 April 1959, p. 4.
A column based on an interview with D.K. Wilgus about three songs concerning the legend of Long John Dean, an escapee from the Warren County jail.

450. Gates, Florence Margaret. "A Study of Living Conditions in the Southern Appalachians as Revealed through the Mountain Ballads." M.A. thesis, Kansas State Teachers College, 1948.
Uses song texts primarily from Appalachian Kentucky as illustrations of the nature of mountain culture. Jean Thomas was a major source of information. Includes many texts but no melodies.

451. Goble, James B. "Gregorian Chanters of Kentucky Hills Sing Music of the Spheres." *In Kentucky* 4, no. 3 (1940): 30-31.
Concerns Edith Fitzpatrick James's organizing of a group of

"mountain patriarchs" to sing religious songs. Compares mountain singing traditions with Gregorian chants.

452. Green, Archie. *Only a Miner: Studies in Recorded Coal Mining Songs.* Urbana: University of Illinois Press, 1972.
"This work is intended as a statement on sound recordings as cultural documents and communicative devices. . . . these songs portray American coal-mining life and reveal miners' values." A major study that contains Kentucky materials.

453. Griffin, Gerald. "26 Pupils, Driver Died Year Ago in Bus Tragedy." *Louisville Courier-Journal,* 27 February 1959, sec. 2, p. 1.
An article on the anniversary of a tragic road accident. Includes a brief note on a locally-composed and sung dirge entitled "There Will Be No School Buses in Heaven."

454. Jackson, George Pullen. *White and Negro Spirituals: Their Life Span and Kinship Tracing 200 Years of Untrammeled Song Making and Singing Among Our Country Folk, with 116 Songs as Sung by Both Races.* Locust Valley, N.Y.: J.J. Augustin, 1944.
A study of the relationships between white spirituals and Afro-American spirituals. Includes a descripton of singing at camp meetings in Kentucky.

455. ———. *White Spirituals in the Southern Uplands.* 1933. Reprint. New York: Dover, 1965.
A discussion of religious folksongs of whites in the southern Appalachians. Includes analysis of melodies. Describes the 1931 *Southern Harmony* singing at Benton.

456. Jameson, Gladys V. "All Glory and Praise to the Ancient of Days." *Mountain Life and Work* 40, no. 2 (1965): 11-12.
An overview of eastern Kentucky sacred songs.

457. ———. "Mountain Ballads." *Mountain Life and Work* 1, no. 3 (1925): 12-19.
An overview of the ballad form, written by a member of the Berea College music faculty.

458. ———. "They Came Singing: A Survey of Sacred Music of the Southern Appalachians, Part I." *Mountain Life and Work* 39, no. 2 (1963): 24-29.
Focuses on the history of musical modes and their relationship to sacred music. [*See also* #459.]

459. ———. "They Came Singing: A Survey of Sacred Music of the Southern Appalachians, Part II." *Mountain Life and Work* 39, no. 3 (1963): 26-31, 34-35.

Deals with the 1820-1840 revivals and the songs that survive from that period. Illustrative texts include tunes.

460. Jansen, William Hugh. " 'Ten Broeck and Molly' and 'The Rose of Kentucky.' " *Kentucky Folklore Record* 4 (1958): 149-53.
    Versions of two songs collected in Princeton, Kentucky, by the author are compared to other versions. No tunes.

461. Krehbiel, Henry Edward. "Kentucky Versions of Some English Ballads." *New York Tribune,* 30 April 1916, section 4.
    A concert by the Edith Rubel Trio sparks the author's discussion of American, particularly Kentucky, folksongs.

462. Leach, MacEdward, and Tristram P. Coffin, eds. *The Critics and the Ballad.* Carbondale: Southern Illinois University Press, 1961.
    An anthology in which several articles cite song texts from, or song scholars active in, Kentucky.

463. Lomax, Alan. *Folk Song Style and Culture.* Washington, D.C.: American Association for the Advancement of Science, 1968.
    One chapter presents the results of a study in which three traditional Kentucky mountain ballads were analyzed and compared to song texts from five other cultures in an attempt to determine the effectiveness of treating song texts as cultural indicators. No texts or tunes.

464. McGill, Anna Blanche. "Historical Elements in the British Ballads Surviving in the Kentucky Mountains." *Kentucky Folk-Lore and Poetry Magazine* 4, no. 2 (1929): 4-12.
    About the historicity of texts collected by Josephine McGill. Ranges in its consideration from classic British ballads to local pieces.

465. ———. "Irish Characteristics in Our Song Survivals." *Musical Quarterly* 18 (1932): 106-19.
    Compares songs collected by Josephine McGill with versions in collections by Irish scholar Dr. P.W. Joyce. Includes at least one text ("The Forsaken Girl") not published by Josephine McGill.

446. McGill, Josephine. "A Quaint Musical Survival: The Twelve Apostles." *Musical Quarterly* 16 (1930): 186-90.
    An essay on a carol-like text collected in Hindman. This version combines song and dialog.

467. ———. "Mountain Minstrelsy." *Berea Quarterly* 9, no. 3 (April 1905): 5-13.
    Points out that extension workers have discovered ancient

British ballads in the mountains and presents several texts, including "Sourwood Mountain" (with melody), versions of Child 73, and "Paper of Pins."

468. ———. "Sing All a Green Willow." *North American Review* 228 (August 1929): 218-24.

An analysis of the appeal, in the Kentucky mountains, of ballads of unhappy romance.

469. Mayans, Anna. "Barbara Allen, the Ballad that Saved a Culture." *Appalachian Heritage* 6, no. 1 (1978): 19-21.

Notes on Olive Dame Campbell's life. Presents a version of "Barbara Allen" as sung by Ada B. Smith in Knott County in 1907. Includes melody.

470. Nelson, Donald Lee. "The Death of J.B. Marcum." *JEMF Quarterly* 11 (1975): 7-22.

A discussion of a ballad generally attributed to Blind Bill Day, recorded first by Chestnut, Martin, and Roberts in 1928, and by other Kentucky artists.

471. Niles, John Jacob. "Folk Ballad and Carol." In *The Great Smokies and the Blue Ridge,* ed. Roderick Peattie. New York: Vanguard Press, 1943.

The author mentions several songs from Kentucky as he discusses folkmusic from the southern mountains.

472. ———. "Shout, Coon, Shout!" *Musical Quarterly* 16 (1930): 516-30.

Afro-American shouts may be divided into two groups—sacred shouts and the shouting of moans, blues, and ballads. Makes a number of references to Kentucky blues singers. Some sample texts are included.

473. ———. *Singing Soldiers.* New York: Charles Scribner's Sons, 1927.

Although primarily about black soldiers and their music during World War I, the book mentions the influence of black spirituals from Kentucky on the author.

474. "Overseas Ballads in Kentucky Valleys." *Review of Reviews* 44 (October 1911): 497-98.

Discusses an article by Hubert G. Shearin in *Sewanee Review* (1911) [see #481] on 37 ballads of English, Scottish, and Irish origin surviving in Kentucky. Quotes extensively from Shearin's article, including partial texts from many of the ballads.

475. Perdue, Frances D. "Folksong Repertoire of Beulah C. Moody." *Kentucky Folklore Record* 22 (1976): 15-24.

Gives examples of ballads, lyrics, religious, and humorous

songs from the repertoire of a Brownsville woman. Fifteen texts; no tunes.

476. Purcell, Janice. " 'Pearl Bryan' and 'The Jealous Lover.' " *Kentucky Folklore Record* 12 (1966): 1-3.
 Compares a Green County version of "Pearl Bryan" with "The Jealous Lover." One text; with music.

477. Raine, James Watt. "The English Ballad." *Mountain Life and Work* 1, no. 1 (1925): 28.
 Some remarks on the use of refrains in ballads. Includes a version of "The Two Sisters." Text only (10 verses).

478. Rexford, Raymond. C. "British Ballads in Our Southern Highlands." *Berea Quarterly* 4, no. 3 (November 1899): 12-14.
 Compares the mountain text of "Lord Bateman, or the Turkish Lady" (Child 53) with the version published by Kinloch. Mentions performances by ballad-singing students at Berea College fundraising events.

479. Roberts, Leonard. "Beauchamp and Sharp: A Kentucky Tragedy." *Kentucky Folklore Record* 14 (1968): 14-19.
 Twenty-three and a half stanzas of a ballad derived from a murder in Frankfort, this version from Bell County. Notes the transformation from fact to ballad.

480. ———. *Sang Branch Settlers: Folksongs and Tales of a Kentucky Mountain Family.* Austin: University of Texas Press, 1974.
 A re-edited version of the author's earlier publications *Up Cutshin and Down Greasy* and *Tales and Songs of the Couch Family.* Contains the song and narrative repertoire of an eastern Kentucky family, with melodies. [See *also* #392.]

481. Shearin, Hubert G. "British Ballads in the Cumberland Mountains." *Sewanee Review* 19 (1911): 313-27.
 Claims that for 200 years isolation in the eastern Kentucky mountains preserved the song traditions of the British Isles. Focuses on 37 songs from the "mother country." Mentions the creation of new songs and also refers to instrumental music. [*See also* #474.]

482. ———. "Kentucky Folksongs." *Modern Language Review* 6 (1911): 513-17.
 Presents full texts, without music, of two ballads from eastern Kentucky which closely parallel the well-known literary works "The Red Red Rose" by Robert Burns and "Glove and Lions" by Leigh Hunt. Raises the question of whether the ballads are the echo or the source of the literary works.

483. Stein, Zonweise. "John Brown's Coal Mine." *Kentucky Folklore Record* 7 (1961): 147-58.
    Examines a song collected from Aunt Molly Jackson.
484. Stewart, Al. "On the Trail of the Great Speckled Bird." *Appalachian Heritage* 6, no. 1 (1978): 67-80.
    A historical consideration of a song the author believes to have been composed in 1926. Includes Kentucky versions. No music.
485. Sutherland, Elihu Jasper. "Vance's Song." *Southern Folklore Quarterly* 4 (1940): 251-54.
    Examines a song composed in Virginia but claimed to be well known in Kentucky and West Virginia as well.
486. Thomas, Jean [Jeannette Bell Thomas]. "The Folk Who Sing Ballads." *Letters* 4, no. 15 (May 1931): 13-17.
    Two ballads sung by Dennis Hall of Rowan County in a September 1911 moonlight school.
487. ———. "How Music Ended a Famous Feud." *Etude* 62 (1944): 96.
    An article about ballad composition in the mountains of Kentucky that presents partial texts of songs about the Civil War, the Spanish-American War, and World War II. The title refers to one song which "shows unity among the once feuding families of Hatfields and McCoys."
488. Thomason, Jean H. "Ten Broeck and Mollie: New Light on a Kentucky Ballad." *Kentucky Folklore Record* 16 (1970): 17-24.
    Compares a version of the ballad collected in 1970 in Grayson County with other texts, including possibly Irish versions. Twenty texts, two with music.
489. Utley, Francis Lee. "The Jug Ballad in Maine and Kentucky." *Southern Folklore Quarterly* 9 (1945): 111-17.
    Concludes that a literary version from Maine was the source for a song collected in Gander, Kentucky.
490. Wells, Evelyn Kendrick. *The Ballad Tree*. New York: Ronald Press, 1950.
    A study of the ballad in Britain and North America. Includes texts collected by the author at Pine Mountain Settlement School and other Kentucky information.
491. Wilgus, D.K. "Down Our Way: Sing Us a Kentucky Song." *Kentucky Folklore Record* 5 (1959): 45-59.
    Presents nine local songs and discusses their significance and transmission.

492. ———. "Fiddler's Farewell: The Legend of the Hanged Fiddler." *Studia Musicologiea* [Academiae Scientiarum Hungaricae] 7 (1965): 195-209.
Many European and American ballad texts include a "last goodnight" involving a fiddler about to be executed. Kentucky texts are used in this discussion of a complex set of ballad relationships. [*See also* #493.]

493. ———. "The Hanged Fiddler Legend in Anglo-American Tradition." *Folklore on Two Continents: Essays in Honor of Linda Degh,* ed. Nikolai Burlakoff and Carl Lindahl. Bloomington, Ind.: Trickster Press, 1980, pp. 120-38.
A study of the "fiddler's farewell" ballad tradition in Western Europe and North America. Includes references to a number of Kentucky texts and instrumental melodies. A revision of the author's article in *Studia Musicologiea* [*see* #492].

494. ———. "Rose Connoley: An Irish Ballad." *Journal of American Folklore* 92 (1979): 172-95.
A discussion of the Irish origins of "Rose Connoley" or "Down in the Willow Garden," which has generally been considered a native American ballad (Laws F6). Includes references to a number of Kentucky texts and singers.

495. ———. "Ten Broeck and Mollie: A Further Note." *Kentucky Folklore Record* 2 (1956): 141-42.
Two fragmentary variants to supplement the author's earlier article [*see* #496.]

496. ———. "Ten Broeck and Mollie: A Race and a Ballad." *Kentucky Folklore Record* 2 (1956): 77-89.
A study of a horse race ballad that compares oral versions with written accounts.

497. ———, and Nathan Hurvitz. " 'Little Mary Phagan': Further Notes on a Native American Ballad in Context." *Journal of Country Music* 4 (1973): 17-30.
Examines a number of variants of Laws F20, including a 1959 fragment from Barren County.

498. ———, and [William] Lynwood Montell. "Beanie Short: A Civil War Chronicle in Legend and Song." In *American Folk Legend: A Symposium,* ed. Wayland D. Hand. Berkeley: University of California Press, 1971.
A ballad and legends about a rebel guerrilla from Monroe and Cumberland counties. Shows how songs and legends can be used to fill gaps in history. Includes melodies.

499. ——— and ———. "Clure and Joe Williams: Legend and Blues Ballad." *Journal of American Folklore* 81 (1968): 295-315.

Deals with the relationship of a local ballad to legend and history. A number of texts, some with music.

500. Williams, Cratis D. "Ballads and Songs." M.A. thesis, University of Kentucky, 1937.

Examines 167 texts from eastern Kentucky, specifically Lawrence County, and analyzes them for similarities to Child ballads. Chapters focus on the history of balladry, ballad structure, play-parties, and dance songs. Includes some melodies.

501. Williams, Richard. " 'Omie Wise': A Cultural Performance." *Kentucky Folklore Record* 23 (1977): 7-11.

Suggests that ballads become popular because of the cultural validity of their performance rather than the authenticity of the events they describe. Based on a study of 40 variants of "Omie Wise."

502. Wilson, O.J. "In Search of a Ballad." *Kentucky Folklore Record* 12 (1966): 108-13.

Presents a murder ballad and a dramatic account of Harlan County's first hanging. No melody.

503. Wolfe, Charles K. "New Light on 'The Coal Creek March.' " *JEMF Quarterly* 12 (1976): 1-8.

A partial history of the transmission of a banjo piece connects it to the lives of a number of Kentucky musicians, including Marion Underwood, Pete Steele, Doc Hopkins, Dick Burnett, and Ernie Hodges.

Studies of History, Context, and Style

Also see entries: #78, 80, 84, 112-13, 160, 214, 309, 329, 334, 368, 392, 405, 425, 442, 444-47, 454-55, 459, 614, 619-21, 625

504. Artis, Bob. *Bluegrass.* New York: Hawthorn, 1975.
A history of bluegrass music concentrating on its major performers. Includes chapters on Kentuckians Bill Monroe and the Osborne Brothers.

505. Ashby, Rickie Zayne. "The Brush Arbor Revival." *Kentucky Folklore Record* 21 (1975): 15-17.
Three verses and the chorus (no music) of a satirical song about a brush arbor revival meeting in Ohio County in 1916; presented as evidence for the thesis that "fervent emotions precipitate the creation of folk music."

506. Boles, John. *The Great Revival, 1787-1805.* Lexington: University Press of Kentucky, 1972.
Traces the origins and development of the religious revival in the South in the early 1800s, with one chapter on the role of hymns in the revival. No texts or tunes.

507. Bourgard, Caroline B. "Public School Music in Kentucky." *Southern School Journal,* October 1925, pp. 22-24.
A history of music in the Kentucky public schools. Includes a reference to a black fiddler who played ca. 1778 on Corn Island.

508. Brewer, Mary T. "A Golden Memory." *Mountain Life and Work* 40, no. 2 (1964): 21-25.
A reminiscence of a summer the author spent with the Ritchie family in Viper, including a description of a family singing session in the evening. No texts or music.

509. Burman-Hall, Linda C. "Southern American Folk Fiddle Styles." *Ethnomusicology* 19 (1975): 47-65.
A revised portion of the author's doctoral dissertation [*see* #510] that attempts to determine some characteristics of traditional fiddle playing and fiddle tunes. Four distinct regional styles of fiddle playing are identified, as determined by comparative analysis of various stylistic factors. No texts or tunes.

510. ———. "Southern American Folk Fiddling: Context and Style." Ph.D. dissertation, Princeton University, 1974.
Surveys the history and context of fiddling in the South and examines 42 versions of two well-known tunes. Identifies four distinct regional styles.

511. Camp, Charles. "The Sound of New Made Old: June Appal Records and Folk Tradition." *Appalachian Journal* 7 (1979-80): 239-48.
Assesses the first 25 releases of June Appal, a recording company in eastern Kentucky specializing in traditional music of Appalachia, and concludes that, on the whole, the label has failed to present an accurate sense of traditional Appalachian music and culture.

512. Carney, George O. "From Down Home to Uptown: The Diffusion of Country-Music Radio Stations in the United States." *Journal of Geography* 76 (1977): 104-10.
Examines diffusion patterns of all-country-music radio stations in the U.S., focusing particularly on the years 1971-1974, and analyzes factors underlying these patterns.

513. ———. "Spatial Diffusion of the All-Country Music Stations in the United States, 1971-74." *JEMF Quarterly* 13 (1977): 58-66.
Finds that all-country-music radio stations generally started in the South and moved outward in all directions. Diffusion followed the migration/relocation of southern people— from south to north and west, from small towns to larger cities.

514. Caudill, Harry M. "Anglo-Saxon vs. Scotch-Irish, Round 2." *Mountain Life and Work* 45, no. 3 (1969): 18-19.
A reply to an article by Tallmadge [see#521] in a previous issue, refuting the theory that Kentucky mountain settlers are of Scotch-Irish background. Says that examining last names is a better way to determine national heritage. This method, as well as ballad study, supports the theory of English ancestry. No texts or music.

515. Chamberlain, William W. "Folk Music in the Kentucky Barrens." M.A. thesis, Stanford University, 1940.
A description of music and music-making in the Barren County area.

516. Chambers, Virginia. "The Hindman Settlement School and Its Music." *Journal of Research in Music Education* 21 (1973): 135-44.

Discusses the impact of the Knott County school's music program on the propagation and dissemination of mountain music.

517. ———. "Music in Four Kentucky Mountain Settlement Schools." Ph.D. dissertation, University of Michigan, 1970.
Examines how four eastern Kentucky schools—Hindman, Pine Mountain, Henderson, and Alice Lloyd College—have dealt with music indigenous to their service areas.

518. Clark, Clarice. "Ballads of Smoky: Hymns and Party Play Songs of Kentucky Mountaineers—Their Texts and Tunes." *New York Times,* 25 August 1929, sec. 8, p. 7.
Describes various religious and recreational activities of Kentucky mountain people: a Sunday meeting, a camp meeting, a play-party. Includes sample texts of religious hymns, "spontaneous composition," and several examples of play-party texts.

519. Clark, Thomas D. "My Old Kentucky Home in Retrospect." *Filson Club History Quarterly* 22 (April 1948): 104-16.
Describes Kentucky culture in the 1800s and suggests that the popularity of Stephen Foster's songs, particularly "My Old Kentucky Home, Good Night," is based on their ability to conjure memories of that bygone era.

520. Coleman, John Winston, Jr. *Slavery Times in Kentucky.* Chapel Hill: University of North Carolina Press, 1940.
Concerns the lives of slaves and their masters in Kentucky. Pages 70-77 deal with spirituals and songs sung at a corn shucking. Presents one stanza from each of 11 songs; no melodies. The song section is based, in part, on a diary written by Judge Cabell Chenault.

521. Creason, Joe. "The Last of the Big Sings." *Louisville Courier-Journal Magazine,* 18 June 1961, pp. 5-7.
Notes on the annual—and enduring—shape-note singing in Benton.

522. Dyen, Doris J. "Symposium on Rural Hymnody." *JEMF Quarterly* 15 (1979): 60-61.
A note on the 1979 conference at Berea College.

523. Epstein, Dena J. *Sinful Tunes and Spirituals: Black Folk Music to the Civil War.* Urbana: University of Illinois Press, 1977.
A major study of black folkmusic before the Civil War. Uses a wide range of original source material.

524. Federal Writers' Project. *Kentucky: A Guide to the Bluegrass State.* American Guide Series. New York: Harcourt, Brace and Co., 1939.

Part of the American Guide Series. Includes a chapter on folklore and folkmusic. Mentions ballads, camp meeting songs, singing schools, black spirituals, play-parties, and instrumental music. Refers to state festivals.

525. Fedric, Francis. *Slave Life in Virginia and Kentucky: or, Fifty Years of Slavery in the Southern States of America.* London: Wertheim, Macintosh, and Hunt, 1863.

Recollections of an escaped slave, containing a chapter on "corn songs" which describes a typical corn shucking, or "bee." Presents the texts of two songs (call and response form).

526. Feintuch, Burt. "A Noncommercial Black Gospel Group in Context: We Live the Life We Sing About." *Black Music Research Journal* 1 (1980): 37-50.

Focusing on a Logan County family group, the article discusses black gospel music as a community-based, rather than commercial, form of music.

527. ———. "Examining Musical Motivation: Why Does Sammie Play the Fiddle?" *Western Folklore* 42 (1983): 208-15.

A discussion of the role of social factors such as family and community as motivation for a south-central Kentucky fiddler who has played for more than 60 years.

528. Fisher, Miles Mark. *Negro Slave Songs in the United States.* Ithaca: Cornell University Press, 1953.

Mentions the singing which accompanied corn husking on a Kentucky plantation.

529. Graham, John R. "Early Twentieth Century Singing Schools in Kentucky Appalachia." *Journal of Research in Music Education* 19 (1971): 77-84.

Describes singing schools on the basis of interviews with former participants, both students and teachers.

530. Green, Archie. "Hillbilly Music: Source and Symbol." *Journal of American Folklore* 78 (1965): 204-28.

An important article legitimizing the study of hillbilly music. Primarily historical.

531. Green, Douglas B. *Country Roots: The Origins of Country Music.* Foreword by Merle Travis. New York: Hawthorn, 1976.

An illustrated history of country music from its European heritage to contemporary Nashville music. Includes many Kentucky musicians, from Bradley Kincaid to Loretta Lynn.

532. Hackney, Alice J. *Cullings of Forty Years, from Musical Lanes and Hedges.* Louisville: Baptist Book Concern, 1910.

Includes notes on the scene at the composition of "My Old Kentucky Home."

533. Horsley, A.D. "The Spatial Impact of White Gospel Quartets in the U.S." *JEMF Quarterly* 15 (1979): 91-98.
    Examines the diffusion pattern of white gospel music from 1920 to 1978 in the United States, based on radio station programming and quartet concert tours. Finds that the music began in southern states, including Kentucky, and spread outward.

534. Hunter, Fanny Middleton. "A Reminiscence." *Kentucky Folk-Lore and Poetry Magazine* 1, no. 3 (1926): 16-17.
    Memories of musical traditions dating from slave days. Includes dance, song, and instrumental music. Written by a Shelbyville resident.

535. Hutchison, Percy. "The Balladry and Folk-Ways of Kentucky Mountaineers." *New York Times Book Review,* 31 January 1932, p. 2.
    A review of *Devil's Ditties* by Jean Thomas [see#567], a book on folkmusic of Kentucky. Includes a few partial song texts.

536. Jackson, George Pullen. "Benton's Big Singings." *Kentucky Progress Magazine* 7 (1936): 94-95, 100.
    A famous scholar of religious song describes the shape-note sing at Benton and gives some history.

537. Jameson, Gladys V. "Music for the Country Children." *Mountain Life and Work* 1, no. 2 (1925): 3-5.
    Discusses the importance of music classes for children in the Appalachian South, referring to special programs having to do with regional identity.

538. ———. "Round Table on Music." *Mountain Life and Work* 2, no. 2 (1926): 35-36.
    An article taken from the minutes of a meeting of the Council of Southern Mountain Workers. Suggests that mountain people should be taught the fine quality of both art songs and their own folkmusic.

539. McGill, Josephine. "The Kentucky Mountain Dulcimer." *Musician* 22 (January 1917): 21.
    A description of the Appalachian dulcimer focusing on its physical dimensions, its tone, and the settings in which it is played. Suggests that the instrument resembles older German zithers.

540. McLain, Raymond K. "Folk Music at Hindman." *Mountain Life and Work* 34, no. 2 (1958): 13-17.

Traces the history of folk music at Hindman Settlement School, discusses the role of the school in keeping alive the traditional music of the region, and the influence of the school on song collectors such as Combs, Sharp, Campbell, and McGill. Includes a description of a singing session at the school. No texts or tunes.

541. MacLean, John Patterson. "The Kentucky Revival and Its Influence on the Miami Valley." *Ohio Archaeological and Historical Publications* 12 (1903): 242-86.
A history of the religious revival that was a major factor in the development of American religious folksong.

542. McNemar, Richard. *The Kentucky Revival.* 1807. Reprint. New York: AMS Press, 1974.
Describes the growth of religious revivalism in Kentucky. Includes a description of camp meeting singing.

543. Malone, Bill C. *Country Music U.S.A.: A Fifty Year History.* Austin: University of Texas Press, 1968.
A pioneering history of country music, with references to Kentucky figures.

544. ———. *Southern Music/American Music.* Lexington: University Press of Kentucky, 1979.
Passing references to early ballad collecting in Kentucky, balladry resulting from 1930s coal strikes in Kentucky, and such Kentucky performers as Buell Kazee, "Grandpa" Jones, Bill Monroe, and Loretta Lynn.

545. Martin, Katherine Rosser. "Cumberland County Singing Convention." *Kentucky Folklore Record* 20 (1974): 29-32.
Contextual treatment of a religious singing convention.

546. Mather, Jay. "Renfro Valley." *Louisville Courier-Journal Magazine,* 27 August 1978, pp. 20-22.
About a famous Rockcastle County music show.

547. Miles, Emma B. *The Spirit of the Mountains.* 1905. Reprint. Knoxville: University of Tennessee Press, 1975.
An early portrait of life in the mountains of Kentucky, Tennessee, and the Carolinas. Includes texts and music for a variety of song genres.

548. Moser, Mabel Y. "Christian Harmony Singing at Etowah." *Appalachian Journal* 1 (1972-73): 263-70.
Focuses on the annual gathering at Etowah, North Carolina, but includes brief references to Kentucky Sacred Harp singing and shape-note hymnals.

549. Moss, Frazier. "The Second Annual Renfro Valley Fiddle Contest." *Devil's Box* 18 (1 September 1972): 4.

A champion fiddler from Tennessee reports on a Kentucky fiddlers contest.

550. Neal, Julia. "Shaker Festival." *Kentucky Folklore Record* 8 (1962): 127-35.

A history of religion at the South Union, Kentucky, Shaker colony. Includes sample stanzas of hymns.

551. Peterson, Richard A., and Russell Davis, Jr. "The Fertile Crescent of Country Music." *Journal of Country Music* 6 (1975): 19-27.

Examines birthplace data for 416 country music performers prominent during the past 50 years and finds that the majority are from the rural South, especially the area from West Virginia to Texas. Kentucky ranks second in ratio of artists to total population.

552. Putnam, John. "The Plucked Dulcimer." *Mountain Life and Work* 34, no. 4 (1958): 7-13.

A history of the southern mountain folk instrument, with biographical information on a number of its builders.

553. ———. *The Plucked Dulcimer and How to Play It.* Berea, Ky.: Council of the Southern Mountains, 1961.

An instruction manual that includes a brief history of the instrument.

554. Rosenberg, Neil. "From Sound to Style: The Emergence of Bluegrass." *Bluegrass Unlimited* 3, no. 7 (January 1969): 6-12.

About the early years of bluegrass music, focusing on Bill Monroe and his influence.

555. ———. "From Sound to Style: The Emergence of Bluegrass." *Journal of American Folklore* 80 (1967): 143-50.

Describes and evaluates the beginnings of bluegrass as a distinctive style of country music, focusing on the role of Bill Monroe.

556. Russell, Tony. *Blacks, Whites and Blues.* New York: Stein and Day, 1970.

Looks at the interaction between black and white folkmusic in America from the 1820s to the 1930s, focusing on minstrel songs, blues, and country music. Some references to Kentucky music and performers.

557. Smith, Betty N. "The Gap in Oral Tradition." In *An Appalachian Symposium: Essays Written in Honor of Cratis D. Williams,* ed. J.W. Williamson. Boone, N.C.: Appalachian State University Press, 1977.

Reports on the decline of the singing tradition in Appalachia.

558. Smith, L. Mayne. "Additions and Corrections." *Bluegrass Un-limited* 1, no. 7 (January 1967): 4-5.
Previously unpublished remarks on the author's earlier article [*see* #560]. Includes notes on a 1965 conversation with Bill Monroe.

559. ————. "An Introduction to Bluegrass." *Bluegrass Unlimited* 1, no. 5 (November 1966): 2-4.
Partial reprint of an article first published in 1965 [#560]. This section deals with the contribution of Rosine native Bill Monroe to the birth of bluegrass music.

560. ————. "An Introduction to Bluegrass." *Journal of American Folklore* 78 (1965): 245-56.
Describes the distinguishing musical and textual charac-teristics of bluegrass music, including its stylistic derivation from Anglo-American folk tradition, and examines the cultural context in which the music is played. Discusses the influence of Kentuckian Bill Monroe in the development of bluegrass.

561. Stewart, Albert F. "Some Things Are Too Beautiful to Die." *Appalachian Heritage* 1, no. 2 (1973): 45-48.
An article about dulcimers, concentrating on Knott County.

562. Stoddard, Hope. "Music in Kentucky." *International Musi-cian* 50, no. 11 (May 1952): 8-10.
Discusses songfests, barn dances, hymn books, singing schools, and the Benton Big Singing.

563. "Students Learn through Music." *Mountain Life and Work* 55, no. 3 (1979): 15.
Describes the efforts of a Kentucky school to foster apprecia-tion for traditional music and promote continuation of the Appalachian heritage.

564. Tallmadge, William H. "Anglo-Saxon vs. Scotch-Irish." *Mountain Life and Work* 45, no. 2 (1969): 10-12.
Suggests that emigration patterns and ballad study indicate that the predominant heritage of the Kentucky mountain area is Scotch-Irish, not English. No song texts or music.

565. Thomas, Jean [Jeannette Bell Thomas]. *Ballad Makin' in the Mountains of Kentucky.* New York: Henry Holt, 1939.
A romanticized acount of folksong in eastern Ken-tucky. Includes texts, sometimes with melodies. Thomas was a well-known author, festival producer, and song collector.

566. ————. *Blue Ridge Country.* Ed. Erskine Caldwell. New York: Duell, Sloan, and Pearce, 1942.
A first-person account of life in Appalachia. Includes sections

on singing and singing schools as well as an association for the preservation of folksinging. Includes texts; no music.

567. ———. *Devil's Ditties.* Chicago: W. Wilbur Hatfield, 1931.
A romanticized account of events in mountain life. Illustrated with song stanzas and a selection of full texts with music.

568. Thomas, William Roscoe. *Life among the Hills and Mountains of Kentucky.* Louisville: Standard Printing Co., 1926.
A history of Kentucky's mountain people that includes a short section describing the songs and musical instruments of the region. The ballad tradition of the mountain people is offered as evidence for their Anglo-Saxon heritage. Claims that dulcimers are on the verge of extinction.

569. Trotter, Margaret. "Singing Berea." *Mountain Life and Work* 7, no. 4 (1932): 9-11.
Looks at the role of music at Berea College throughout the school's history, including numerous choral groups and glee clubs which have often had traditional ballads and hymns as an important part of their repertoire. No texts or tunes.

570. Wellman, Lester R. "Down on the Quiet Levee, A Roustabout Strikes a Tune." *Louisville Courier-Journal Magazine,* 25 August 1957, pp. 60-61.
A description of a typical day in Louisville in the 1890s, including a description of an Afro-American banjo player and fragments of his repertoire.

571. Wells, Evelyn K. "Ballad Backgrounds in the Appalachians." *Mountain Life and Work* 23, no. 3 (1947): 14-18, 23-24.
Describes how the lifestyle of mountain people has been favorable to the preservation and survival of ballads. Contains stanzas from a few songs but no musical transcriptions.

572. Williams, Cratis D. "The Southern Mountaineer in Fact and Fiction (Part IV) Chapter 9: 'Hillbilly! Hillbilly!'" [Edited by Martha H. Pipes]. *Appalachian Journal* 3 (1975-76): 358-78.
Points out that much of the material in Jean Thomas's books is romanticized nostalgia.

573. Wolfe, Charles K. *Kentucky Country: Folk and Country Music of Kentucky.* Lexington: University Press of Kentucky, 1982.
Examines Kentucky's contribution to country music, focusing on the transformation of grassroots music to commercial music. Includes a useful selected discography.

574. ———. "Toward a Contextual Approach to Old-Time Music." *Journal of Country Music* 5 (1974): 65-75.
Discusses prevailing artist- and song-oriented approaches to

the study of early commercial recordings of old-time music. Suggests a broader contextual approach focusing on the artist-company relationship, discographic data, the role of the records in society, and the effect on the artist. Musician Dick Burnett, of Monticello, is mentioned.

575. Wood, Henry Cleveland. "Negro Camp-Meeting Melodies." In *The Social Implications of Early Negro Music in the United States,* ed. Bernard Katz. New York: Arno Press, 1969.
The author, who grew up near Harrodsburg, describes Afro-American camp meetings held in his youth. Includes six song texts with melodies.

576. Woolley, Bryan. "The Hodgenville Sound." *Louisville Courier-Journal and Times Magazine,* 18 March 1973, pp. 18-22.
About Saturday night country music shows at the Lincoln Jamboree in Hodgenville.

577. "Would You Believe?" *Devil's Box* 21 (1 June 1973): 17.
A reprint of a 1927 *Nashville Tennessean* article on a fiddlers' contest at Oakland, Warren County.

578. Young, Chester Raymond. "The Observance of Old Christmas in Southern Appalachia." In *An Appalachian Symposium: Essays Written in Honor of Cratis D. Williams,* ed. by J.W. Williamson. Boone, N.C.: Appalachian State University Press, 1977.
Includes information on the role of caroling in the celebration of Old Christmas, with samples of Kentucky versions of "The Cherry Tree Carol."

Festivals

Also see entries: #214, 277, 314, 356, 400, 524, 629, 631

579. "American Folk Song Festival." *Arcadian Life* 2 (June 1935): 7-8.
An announcement of the upcoming fifth annual festival, with notes on Jilson Setters, the festival's "drawing power." Includes two texts, words only, for songs attributed to Setters. With photographs.

580. "American Folk Song Festival Will Be Revived June 9." *In Kentucky* 10, no. 1 (Spring 1946): 30-31.
On the first of Jean Thomas's festivals to be held after a moratorium during World War II. Includes photographs and notes on performers.

581. "Bow with Antic Ways Puts Hillbilly Fiddler at Top of Bill." *Newsweek* 5 (18 May 1935): 20.
Background on Sarah Gertrude Knott's second National Folk Festival in Chattanooga and on featured performer Jilson Setters. With text of the "Cherry Tree Carol" and photograph.

582. Brandeis, Fanny. "Another Singin' Day Is Drawing Near." *Kentucky Progress Magazine* 7 (1936): 120-21.
Tells the story of the establishment by Jean Thomas of the American Folk Song Festival. Describes some of the common mountain instruments and the "Fireside Singin' Gatherin's" held in the winter in Thomas's home as preparation for the annual summer festival.

583. "Echoes from the Folk Festival." *Mountain Life and Work* 15, no. 2 (1939): 24-26.
A review of the fourth Mountain Folk Festival held in Berea in April 1939. Includes program, photographs, and extracts from letters praising the event.

584. Field, Richard. "A Bit of Olde England: The Traipsin' Woman Presents Another Singin' Festival at Ashland." *Louisville Courier-Journal Magazine,* 17 July 1960, pp. 10-15.
A description of the thirtieth annual American Folk Song Festival near Ashland and a profile of the festival's founder, Jean Thomas. No song texts or music.

585. "Folk Song Lovers to Attend 13th Festival in Jolt Wagons." *In Kentucky* 7, no. 1 (Spring 1943): 42, 47.
A short article on the upcoming American Folk Song Festival. Lists a number of participants and is illustrated with photograph of performing members of the Hatfield and Mc-Coy families.

586. Hardaway, Howard. "Sparked by Kentuckians." *Louisville Courier-Journal Magazine,* 14 May 1961, pp. 56, 58, 60.
Background on Kentuckian Sarah Gertrude Knott and the National Folk Festival, which she founded. Includes notes on festival participants from Kentucky. With photographs.

587. "Hatfields and McCoys Famous Feudin' Families Sing—and Forget to Fight." *In Kentucky* 6, no. 1 (Spring 1942): 23.
A brief piece on the upcoming twelfth annual American Folk Song Festival. Illustrated with a photograph featuring Jilson Setters, Jean Thomas, and other performers.

588. "Highlanders Music Workshop." *Mountain Life and Work* 54, no. 11 (1978): 37.
A brief note on a coal mining music workshop held in honor of former United Mine Workers organizers Jim Garland and Sam Reese.

589. Kennedy, Paul. "Minstrels of the Kentucky Hills." *Travel* 79 (June 1942): 14-15ff.
An overview of Jean Thomas's American Folk Song Festival near Ashland. With photographs.

590. "Knott Students Present Medley of Folk Songs, Dances, Games." *Louisville Courier-Journal,* 1 December 1960, sec. 2, p. 1.
A review of a Louisville performance by teenagers from Hindman Settlement School.

591. "Muhlenburgers to Honor 'Sixteen Tons' and 'Admiral' Travis Friday June 29." *Central City* [Kentucky] *Times-Argus,* 28 June 1956, p. 1.
A report on activities to take place as part of ceremonies honoring Merle Travis, Muhlenburg County native.

592. Ogren, Ruth. "The American Folk Song Festival." *Kentucky Progress Magazine* 6 (1935): 336-37.
A romantic perspective on the festival organized by Jean Thomas. Includes photographs.

593. ———. "Third Annual American Folk Song Festival." *Kentucky Progress Magazine* 5, no. 4 (1933): 36-37.
Notes on an important early festival held near Ashland.

594. "Ohio Singer, Bagpipes Star at Ashland Folk Festival."
Louisville Courier-Journal, 12 June 1961, sec. 2, p. 1.
A brief note on the thirty-first annual American Folk Song
Festival.
595. Russell, Tony. "Big Ball in Montreal." *Old Time Music* 2 (Autumn 1971): 4-7.
A festival held in Montreal includes Kentucky performers
such as Bill Williams and the Coon Creek Girls. With photographs.
596. "Second National Folk Song Festival." *Newsweek* 5 (18 May
1935): 20.
A short piece on the festival.
597. "Singin' Gatherin'." *Time* 31 (20 June 1938): 25.
A review of the eighth annual American Folk Song Festival
attended by 6,000.
598. "Singin' Gatherin'." *Time* 39 (22 June 1942): 44.
A short review of the twelfth annual American Folk Song
Festival. Includes a fragment of the "Ballad of Alvin York."
599. Smith, Hazel. "Monroe Homecoming." *Bluegrass Unlimited*
8, no. 5 (November 1973): 19.
Notes on an Ohio County bluegrass festival sponsored by Bill
Monroe.
600. Thomas, Dorothy. "That Traipsin' Woman." *Independent Woman* 13 (June 1934): 169, 188-89.
An article based on an interview with Jean Thomas. Focuses
on her involvement with mountain people and the American
Folk Song Festival. With photographs.
601. Thomas, Jean [Jeannette Bell Thomas]. "The American Folk
Song Festival." *Register of the Kentucky State Historical Society* 65, no. 1 (1967): 20-27.
Thomas recounts the occasion on which she discovered a
"Singin' Gatherin'" in the Kentucky mountains and describes
how that centuries-old tradition evolved into the annual American Folk Song Festival. No texts or tunes.
602. ———. "Singin' Fiddler Invites King and Queen to Folk Song
Festival." *In Kentucky* 3, no. 1 (Spring 1939): 33, 46.
On the background and line-up for the "Ninth Annual Singin'
Gatherin'"—the American Folk Song Festival. With photographs.
603. ———. "The Singin' Gatherin'." *American Antiques Journal*
4 (June 1949): 20-22.
A romanticized account of a local singing event which was

transformed into the author's American Folk Song Festival. Essentially the same as the citation below [#604].

604. ———. "The Singin' Gatherin'." *Kentucky School Journal* 16, no. 5 (January 1938): 13-17.
The author's discovery of music in the mountains and the beginning of her American Folk Song Festival.

605. ———. "Twelfth Annual American Folk Song Festival." *Kentucky School Journal* 20, no. 9 (May 1942): 33-35.
Notes on the upcoming festival.

606. ———. "When Singin' Comes In, Fightin' Goes Out." *Musical Digest* 30 (March 1948): 8, 31.
At the seventeenth annual American Folk Song Festival, members of the feuding Hatfield and McCoy families perform together in a musical drama based on the episode which is said to have precipitated the feud.

607. "Traipsin' Woman Gives 26th Festival of Mountain Folk Songs at Ashland." *Louisville Courier-Journal,* 11 June 1956, p. 13.
Fifteen hundred people attend the three-hour program. Includes notes on performers.

608. "Voices of the Hills: Traipsin' Woman Is Rallying Kentucky Minstrels Again." *Newsweek,* 6 June 1938, p. 24.
A brief article about the 1938 folk festival in Boyd County.

609. Welch, Rob. "Appalachian Festival Draws Record Crowd." *Mountain Life and Work* 54, no. 5 (1978): 22-26.
Describes a Cincinnati festival of traditional Appalachian music and crafts featuring some Kentucky performers.

610. Wilgus, D.K. "Singin' Gatherin'." *Columbus* [Ohio] *Sunday Dispatch Magazine,* 19 June 1949, pp. 24-27.
Reportedly an illustrated article on the 1948 American Folk Song Festival in Kentucky. Copy not available for verification of citation or annotation.

Dance

Also see entries: #192, 500

611. "Ambassadors of Good Will." *Berea Alumnus* (January-February 1976): 8-10.
    About the Berea Country Dancers' 1975 tour of England and Scotland.
612. Blair, Kathryn. "Swing Your Partner!" *Journal of American Folklore* 40 (1927): 96-99.
    A note on dancing in "backwoods districts" in Kentucky. Includes a description of events and texts for play-party songs. No melodies.
613. "'Circle Left' Again Available." *Mountain Life and Work* 30, no. 2 (1954): 20.
    Announces reissue of *Circle Left* [see#192], a book of games played by school children in mountain schools. Includes text, musical notation, and directions for one game, "Bluebird, Bluebird," included in the collection.
614. Clark, Thomas D. *The Kentucky.* New York: Farrar and Rinehart, 1942.
    An account of the Kentucky River country in eastern Kentucky. Includes descriptions of bran dances, religious folksongs (especially "hard-shell" Baptist), and a "gay party" featuring a German musician.
615. Coats, Ida Symmes. "Aunt Eliza and Her Slaves." *Kentucky Folk-Lore and Poetry Magazine* 2, no. 2 (1927): 2-6.
    Includes a description of square dance calling in Louisville and partial texts of slave songs.
616. Dean, Jeanette Cope. "Berea College Fosters Traditional Folk Games." *In Kentucky* 8, no. 1 (Spring 1944): 33, 50.
    Traces the development of Berea's institutional interest in folk games and dances as recreation. Illustrated.
617. Drake, Daniel. *Letters on Slavery to Dr. John C. Warren of Boston.* New York: Schumans, 1940.
    Includes a description of a slave dance in Kentucky (pp. 16-17).

618. Duke, Jerry. "Appalachian Clog Dancing—Exciting and Challenging." *Journal of Physical Education and Recreation* 49, no. 9 (1978): 73-75.
Discusses the revival of interest in Appalachian-style clog dancing throughout the U.S. Does not discuss the music.

619. Emery, Lynne Fauley. *Black Dance in the United States from 1619-1970*. Palo Alto: National Press Books, 1972.
Includes a description by an ex-slave of black dancing and music accompanying quilting on a Kentucky plantation.

620. Feintuch, Burt. "Dancing to the Music: Domestic Square Dances and Community in Southcentral Kentucky (1880-1940)." *Journal of the Folklore Institute* 18 (1981): 49-68.
Reconstruction of community square dance traditions based on interviews with callers, dancers, and musicians in southcentral Kentucky. Suggests that the dances embody community and individual values.

621. Friedland, LeeEllen. "Traditional Folkdance in Kentucky." *Country Dance and Song* 10 (1979): 5-19.
Discusses the importance of traditional dancing as a social event in rural Kentucky communities. Describes the music used as accompaniment as well as the musicians and their instruments.

622. Gadd, May. "Pine Mountain Folk Art." *Dance Observer* 5 (1938): 146.
On the occasion of Pine Mountain Settlement School's Silver Jubilee, students perform mountain dance and song, apparently at the Brooklyn Museum. With photograph.

623. Gray, Florence. "Folk Dancing in Letcher County." *Mountain Life and Work* 29, no. 1 (1953): 26-27.
A history of folk dance teams (revivalist dance groups) in one county.

624. Gunkler, Oscar H. "A Dance Drama of Kentucky." *Journal of Physical Education* 7 (March 1936): 157-59.
Describes a dance program dealing with events in the history of Kentucky. Uses folksongs.

625. Harzoff, Elizabeth Gail. "They'd Have the Biggest Time You Ever Saw: Square Dances as Settings for Community Social Interaction in Trigg County, Kentucky, ca. 1920-1979." M.A. thesis, Western Kentucky University, 1981.
Examines the role of neighborhood dances, play-parties, picnics and barbecues, and public dances. Includes a description

of a typical dance band, the type of music played, etc. Words to one play-party song, "Swing Old Betty," provided. Attributes the decline in the number of local musicians playing traditional square dance music to the decline of public dances.

626. Jacobs, Adam. "American Play Stuff: Party Plays." *Theatre Arts* 15 (March 1931): 247-50.
Presents play-party songs, describes the "dances" and the context of the songs. No melodies.

627. Katona, Arthur, and Betsy Bankart. "Christmas Dance School: Two Impressions." *Mountain Life and Work* 22, no. 1 (1946): 17-19.
Notes on the 1945 edition of the country dance school held at Berea College.

628. Levin, Ida. *Kentucky Square Dances.* Louisville: Recreation Council, 1928.
A 31-page booklet with descriptions of, and instructions for, 21 dances. Includes a list of titles particularly well-liked by fiddlers as accompaniment for the dances. No texts or musical transcriptions.

629. "Louisvillians Polish Up Square Dancing for National Convention Here in June." *Louisville Courier-Journal*, 2 January 1958, sec. 1, n.p.
Louisville to host the National Square Dance Convention, expected to draw 10,000 western-style dancers.

630. Napier, Patrick E. "'Old Side Door': A Kentucky Mountain Dance." *Mountain Life and Work* 25, no. 2 (1949): 23-25.
Describes a dance from Perry County. Based on the author's personal experience.

631. Nauss, Jane Bishop. "Festival Draws Two Hundred Dancers." *Mountain Life and Work* 29, no. 2 (1953): 21.
A report on a festival associated with Berea.

632. *Notes from the Pine Mountain Settlement School* 11, no. 1 (1938), unpaginated.
Brief mention of a dance in England learned originally at Pine Mountain school.

633. "Old Tucker." *Mountain Life and Work* 29, no. 2 (1953): 22-23.
Instructions for a dance from Perry County.

634. Peterson, Barbara J. "A Bibliographical Essay on the Adult Literature of the Folk Dance of Southern Appalachia." M.S. thesis, Palmer Graduate Library School, 1972.
Through research and observation concerning dance in the

southern Appalachians, Peterson concludes that "there is an extensive amount of material of historical and cultural value."

635. Pullen, Carl W. "Some More Dance Songs from West Kentucky." *Kentucky Folk-Lore and Poetry Magazine* 3, no. 1 (1928): 15-18.
Texts only; no notes.

636. Sanders, J.O. "Finding List of Southeastern Square Dance Figures." *Southern Folklore Quarterly* 6 (1942): 263-76.
A bibliography and finding list of square dance figures. Includes over 70 Kentucky examples.

637. Sharp, Cecil J., and Maud Karpeles. *The Country Dance Book, Part V: Containing the Running Set.* London: Novello and Co., 1918.
A historic description of square dance figures as observed in the vicinity of Hyden, Hindman, and Pine Mountain.

638. Smith, Frank H. "Christmas Dance School." *Mountain Life and Work* 28, no. 3 (1952): 26.
An announcement for, and program of, the Fifteenth Annual Christmas Country Dance School at Berea. No song texts or music.

639. ———. "Dances and Singing Games." In *The Southern Appalachian Region: A Survey,* ed. Thomas R. Ford. Lexington: University of Kentucky Press, 1962.
Reports on some traditional square dances and play-party games still common throughout the southern Appalachian region. Describes efforts to preserve the folk culture of the region, including the Berea College Mountain Folk Festival.

640. ———. "The Running Set." *Mountain Life and Work* 27, no. 3 (1951): 34.
A note on Cecil Sharp's popularizing the running set. Quotes from Sharp's account of the dance at Pine Mountain.

641. ———, and Rolf E. Hovey. *The Appalachian Square Dance.* Berea, Ky.: Berea College, 1955.
The background and history of Appalachian dancing. Includes dance calls and 19 dance tunes.

642. Smith, John F. "Plays and Games." *Kentucky Folk-Lore and Poetry Magazine* 1, no. 4 (1927): 9-14.
Texts to accompany singing games. With instructions.

643. Stuart, Jesse. "Kentucky Hill Dance." *New Republic* 79 (16 May 1934): 15-16.
Whiskey, fighting, and fiddling at a local square dance.

644. "U.K. Collection Contains over 60 Folk Dances." *Louisville Courier-Journal,* 1 February 1959, sec. 1, p. 26.
A short description of a folk dance booklet compiled by the Co-operative Extension Service at the University of Kentucky.

645. Williamson, Billie. "Fun and Games of Mountain Children." *Kentucky Folklore Record* 21 (1975): 43-55.
Describes several singing games from eastern Kentucky. Includes texts.

646. Wilson, Gordon. "Breakdowns." *Mountain Life and Work* 1, no. 3 (1925): 20-25.
A discussion of breakdowns, both those that are sung and those that are only played on a musical instrument. Includes stanzas from a few sung breakdowns but no musical transcriptions.

647. ———. "Singing Games or Play-Party Games." *Bulletin of the Kentucky Folk-Lore Society* (1925): 26-30.
Claims that such games are extinct in places other than the mountains.

Discographies, Checklists, and Other Specialized Reference Tools

Also see entries: #258, 314, 316, 318, 340, 346, 351-52, 359, 378, 573, 634, 636

648. "Appendix E: A Selected Bibliography of Unpublished Theses and Dissertations." *Appalachian Journal* 5 (1977): 169-75.
   Has a section on folklore and music.

649. *Check-list of Recorded Songs in the English Language in the Archive of American Folk Song to July 1940.* 3 vols. Washington, D.C.: Library of Congress, Music Division, 1942.
   A list of field recordings (1933-1940) in the Archive of American Folk Song (now Archive of Folk Culture) at the Library of Congress. Includes more than 1,000 Kentucky recordings. Citations include informant, place, and collector.

650. Cohen, Norm. "Computerized Hillbilly Discography: The Gennett Project." *Western Folklore* 30 (1971): 182-93.
   Describes the author's project, funded by the National Endowment for the Humanities, to computerize a discography of Gennett, a Richmond, Indiana, label which issued many early hillbilly records. Mentions Kentucky musicians who recorded for the company, including the Tweedy Brothers, Doc Roberts, Edgar Boaz, and Welby Toomey.

651. Coleman, John Winston, Jr. *A Bibliography of Kentucky History.* Lexington: University of Kentucky Press, 1949.
   Has a section on music and songs.

652. ———. *Kentucky Rarities: A Check List of One Hundred and Thirty-Five Fugitive Books and Pamphlets Relating to the Bluegrass State and Its People.* Lexington, Ky.: Winburn Press, 1970.
   An annotated bibliography of hard-to-come-by titles on the history of Kentucky. Some of the items may contain information relating to folkmusic.

653. ———. *Scarce Kentuckiana: A Check List of One Hundred Uncommon and Significant Books and Pamphlets Relating to the Bluegrass State and Its People.* Lexington, Ky.: Winburn Press, 1970.
None of the 100 items is about music specifically, but all are accounts of life in early Kentucky and some may contain information on music.

654. "Discography of Recordings by Buell Kazee." *JEMF Quarterly* 6 (1970): 19-22.
Covers the period 19 April 1927, through 24 July 1929. Also includes information on reissues.

655. Earle, Gene. "Discography—Cliff and Bill Carlisle." *Folk Style* 7 (n.d.): 7-21.
Lists the recordings of both brothers from Richmond, together and with various performing ensembles. [See *also* #318.]

656. Eller, Ronald D. "Dissertations on the Appalachian South." *Appalachian Notes* 3 (1975): 1-6.
A selected guide to relevant dissertations.

657. Epstein, Dena J. "Slave Music in the United States before 1860: A Survey of Sources, Parts I-II." *Music Library Association Notes* 20 (1963): 195-212, 377-90.
Concerns sources for references to slave music, singing, dancing, and musical instruments. Includes musical examples.

658. Feintuch, Burt. "The Fiddle in North America: Recent Recordings." *Journal of American Folklore* 95 (1982): 493-500.
A review essay that includes discussion of recordings by a number of Kentucky fiddlers released on the three-volume set entitled *Old-Time Fiddle Band Music from Kentucky* (Morningstar 45003, 45004, 45005).

659. Fuld, James J. *A Pictorial Bibliography of the First Editions of Stephen C. Foster.* Philadelphia: Musical Americana, 1957.
Describes and provides bibliographic data on first editions of 204 compositions by Foster. Includes original illustrations as well as some texts and tunes.

660. Green, Archie. "An Aunt Molly Jackson Discography." *Kentucky Folklore Record* 7 (1961): 159-69.
A list of recordings by Aunt Molly Jackson. Part of a memorial issue.

661. Healy, Bob, comp. "The Prairie Ramblers." *Country Directory* 3 (n.d.): 4-14.
A discography covering the period 1932-1947. The introduc-

tion outlines the background of the band originally comprised of Kentucky natives and first called the Kentucky Ramblers.

662. Henry, Mellinger Edward. *A Bibliography for the Study of American Folk-Songs*. London: Mitre Press, n.d.
A bibliography that includes Kentucky references.

663. Jones, Loyal. "Bradley Kincaid Discography." *JEMF Quarterly* 12 (1976): 223-28.
Covers 1927-1973.

664. ———. "A Checklist of Bradley Kincaid's Songs." *JEMF Quarterly* 12 (1976): 212-22.
Derived from Kincaid's records and songbooks. Each song is presented with brief comments from Kincaid and short annotations.

665. Kahn, Ed. "Hillbilly Music: Source and Resource." *Journal of American Folklore* 78 (1965): 257-66.
A bibliographic essay on the literature of country music, both academic and popular publications, especially those dealing with the commercial recording industry. Kahn contends this area has been neglected and encourages that in-depth, scholarly studies be undertaken. Some references to Kentucky performers.

666. Knott, Sarah Gertrude. *Kentucky Lore: A Gatherin' of Mountain Music, Songs, and Dances*. Frankfort: Kentucky Council of the Performing Arts and Kentucky Department of Commerce, 1963.
"This booklet is intended for use by those who need a simple guide in their search for folk singers, dancers, and tale tellers in Kentucky." A finding list written by the founder of the National Folk Festival.

667. Laws, G. Malcolm. *American Balladry from British Broadsides*. Philadelphia: American Folklore Society, 1957.
Classifies broadside ballads by types, analyzes their relation to Child ballads, and discusses forms and variants. Presents a bibliography of each ballad, a sample stanza, and a summary of its story. Some Kentucky references.

668. ———. *Native American Balladry: A Descriptive Study and a Bibliographical Syllabus*. Philadelphia: American Folklore Society, 1964.
Classifies ballads of American origin into nine categories based on subject matter. Summarizes each ballad, gives a sample stanza, and provides bibliographical data for printed texts and detailed studies. Includes Kentucky citations.

669. Lloyd, Timothy Charles. "Early Folk Festivals in America: An Introduction and Bibliography." *JEMF Quarterly* 14 (1978): 94-105.

A short analysis of articles, written by Sarah Gertrude Knott for the journal *Recreation,* on folk festivals and uses of folkloric materials in them. Accompanied by a bibliography of literature on folk festivals to be found in non-folklore publications, including ten articles by Knott and several about Jean Thomas and the American Folk Song Festival in Kentucky.

670. Lowens, Irving. *A Bibliography of Songsters Printed in America before 1821.* Worcester: American Antiquarian Society, 1976.

Two of the songsters are volumes of masonic songs from the Grand Lodge of Kentucky. No other Kentucky material.

671. McCuen, Brad. "Monroe Brothers Discography." *Bluegrass Unlimited* 4, no. 6 (December 1969): 8-9.

Recordings from 1936-1938, by the Ohio County duet, Bill and Charlie.

672. McMurtrie, Douglas C., and Albert H. Allen. *Checklist of Kentucky Imprints, 1787-1810.* American Imprints Inventory, no. 5. Louisville: Historical Records Survey, 1939.

Contains citations for early hymnals.

673. ———. *Checklist of Kentucky Imprints, 1811-1820.* American Imprints Inventory, no. 6. Louisville: Historical Records Survey, 1939.

A list of 429 broadsides, pamphlets, and books from Kentucky, with information on libraries and private collections where they are located. Includes some hymnals.

674. McNeil, W.K. "Southern Folk Music on Records." *Southern Exposure* 5, no. 2-3 (1977): 178-86.

Surveys record companies offering southern folk music, both by traditional performers and by revivalists, and describes some significant releases. Includes a number of Kentucky performers.

675. Miles, Virginia. "Kentucky Literary Magazines since 1900." M.A. thesis, Western Kentucky State Teachers College, 1935.

Notes on the *Kentucky Folk-Lore and Poetry Magazine* and its publication of the work of Josephine McGill.

676. "Music in the Mountains." *Mountain Life and Work* 33, no. 2 (1957): 15.

Announces records and books available from the Council of the Southern Mountains, Inc.

677. Niles, John Jacob. "Music." *Mountain Life and Work* 12, no. 2 (1936): 23-24.
A bibliography for those interested in folkmusic.
678. Perrin, Alfred H. "News and Notes." *Appalachian Notes* 2, no. 1 (1974): 12.
Describes material in the Weatherford-Hammond Appalachian Collection in Berea College library, including a 23-page manuscript of folksongs collected by Katherine Jackson French before 1910.
679. ———. "Southern Appalachian Mountain Lore: Berea College's Weatherford-Hammond Mountain Collection." *Appalachia* 6 (April-May 1973): 36-39.
Describes the holdings of the collection, including some 350 books on ballads, and records and tapes of traditional music. Discusses the activities of the college and uses of the collection. No texts or tunes.
680. Rhodes, Willard. "Maud Karpeles Bibliography." *Ethnomusicology* 21 (1977): 285-88.
Lists the works of Cecil Sharp's companion, editor, and biographer as well as a moving force in the International Folk Music Council.
681. "Roberts-Martin-Roberts Discography." Pts. I-V. *JEMF Quarterly* 7 (1971): 103-4, 158-62; 8 (1972): 15-17, 73-76.
A thorough listing of the recordings of Doc Roberts, James Roberts, and Asa Martin along with their varied musical associates.
682. Rosenberg, Neil. *Bill Monroe and His Blue Grass Boys: An Illustrated Discography.* Nashville: Country Music Foundation Press, 1974.
A discography of recordings by the Rosine native, founder of bluegrass music, and his band. Includes a biographical sketch.
683. ———. "Osborne Brothers Discography." *Bluegrass Unlimited* 1, no. 12 (June 1967): 2-5. [*See also* #684-85.]
Lists early recordings, 1950-1956, of the bluegrass musicians from Hyden.
684. ———. "The Osborne Brothers Discography—Part II." *Bluegrass Unlimited* 2, no. 1 (July 1967): 6-8.
Recordings, 1956-1963.
685. ———. "The Osborne Brothers Discography, Part III." *Bluegrass Unlimited* 2, no. 3 (September 1967): 2-3.
Recordings, 1963-1966.
686. Russell, Tony. "The Recordings of A.G. Karnes." *Old Time Music* 7 (Winter 1972-73): 20.

A discography of the Corbin area religious singer-guitarist who recorded in 1927-1928.

687. Sakol, Jeannie. *The Wonderful World of Country Music.* New York: Grosset and Dunlap, 1979.
An illustrated encyclopedia of performers, publications, organizations, events, and miscellanea about country music. Includes some references to Kentucky.

688. Shearin, Hubert G., and Josiah H. Combs. *A Syllabus of Kentucky Folk-Songs.* Lexington: Transylvania Printing Co., 1911.
A guide for comparison and identification of Kentucky folksongs. Deals primarily with eastern and central Kentucky.

689. Spottswood, Richard K. "The Commercial Recordings of Charlie Monroe." *Bluegrass Unlimited* 3, no. 11 (May 1969): 3-6.
A discography spanning the years 1938-1964.

690. Thomason, Jean H. *Shaker Manuscript Hymnals from South Union, Kentucky.* Kentucky Folklore Series, no. 3. Bowling Green: Kentucky Folklore Society, 1967 (mimeographed).
Descriptions of 15 manuscript hymnals from the Shaker community in South Union. The hymnals are in the collection of the Kentucky Library at Western Kentucky University.

691. Whisnant, David E. "Thicker Than Fiddlers in Hell: Issues and Resources in Appalachian Music." *Appalachian Journal* 5 (1977-78): 103-15.
Reviews the scholarship on Appalachian music, suggesting areas needing further study. Offers a guide to resources available and recommends approaches to continued study. Includes some Kentucky references.

692. Wilgus, D.K. *Anglo-American Folksong Scholarship since 1898.* New Brunswick, N.J.: Rutgers University Press, 1959.
A major history of scholarship that includes discussions of work done in Kentucky.

693. ———. "A Syllabus for Kentucky Folksongs." *Kentucky Folklore Record* 1 (1955): 31-38.
On the need for a guide to song texts from Kentucky. Includes notes on the history of song scholarship and on classification.

694. ———. "Discography—1963-1964." *Kentucky Folklore Record* 11 (1965): 9-11.
Eighteen citations.

695. ———. "Discography: 1965." *Kentucky Folklore Record* 12 (1966): 21-23.
Twenty-seven citations.

696. ———. "Discography: 1966." *Kentucky Folklore Record* 13 (1967): 11-12.
Sixteen entries.

697. ———. "Discography of Kentucky Folklore for 1967." *Kentucky Folklore Record* 14 (1968): 20-21.
Eighteen citations.

698. ———. "Discography of Kentucky Folklore for 1968." *Kentucky Folklore Record* 14 (1968): 100-102.
Nineteen citations and a footnote concerning the author's standards for inclusion.

699. ———. "Kentucky Discography, 1969." *Kentucky Folklore Record* 16 (1970): 7-10.
Twenty-seven citations.

700. ———. "Kentucky Discography, 1970." *Kentucky Folklore Record* 17 (1971): 63-64.
Fifteen citations.

701. ———. "The Josiah H. Combs Collection of Songs and Rhymes." *Kentucky Folklore Record* 6 (1960): 125-36.
A partial list of titles from Combs's collection, with annotations.

702. Wolfe, Charles K. "Richard Burnett Discography." *Old Time Music* 12 (Spring 1974): 32.
Recording information spanning 1926-1930 for the Monticello fiddler.

703. Woodbridge, Hensley C., and D.K. Wilgus. "Bibliography of Kentucky Folklore for 1956." *Kentucky Folklore Record* 3 (1957): 17-28.
Contains a discography.

704. ——— and ———. "Folklore Bibliography for 1957." *Kentucky Folklore Record* 4 (1958): 15-28.
Contains a discography.

705. ——— and ———. "Folklore Bibliography for 1958." *Kentucky Folklore Record* 5 (1959): 15-31.
Contains a discography.

706. ——— and ———. "Folklore Bibliography for 1959." *Kentucky Folklore Record* 6 (1960): 21-30.
Contains a discography.

707. ——— and ———. "Bibliography of Kentucky Folklore for 1960." *Kentucky Folklore Record* 7 (1961): 23-33.
Contains a discography.

708. ——— and ———. "Bibliography of Kentucky Folklore for 1961." *Kentucky Folklore Record* 8 (1962): 21-28.
Contains a discography.

709. ———— and ————. "Bibliography of Kentucky Folklore for 1962." *Kentucky Folklore Record* 9 (1963): 29-36.
Contains a discography.

Index of Authors

Entries are indexed by citation number

Subject Index

Entries are indexed by citation number

Index of Periodicals Cited

Entries are indexed by citation number